"THE MOVIE THAT CHANGED MY LIFE"

"THE MOVIE THAT CHANGED MY LIFE"

120 Celebrities Pick the Films

That Made a Difference

(For Better or Worse)

By Robert Hofler
with additional profiles by
Anna Stewart, Stuart Levine,
Peter Debruge, and Andrew Barker

DA CAPO PRESS
A Member of the Perseus Books Group

To Steven Gaydos

Library of Congress Cataloging-in-Publication Data

Hofler, Robert.
  Variety's "the movie that changed my life" : 120 celebrities pick the films that made a difference (for better or worse) / by Robert Hofler. — 1st Da Capo press ed.
      p. cm.
  ISBN 978-0-7867-2100-9 (alk. paper)
  1. Motion pictures. 2. Celebrities—United States—Miscellanea. I. Title.
  PN1994.H59 2009
  791.43'75—dc22
                                                                    2008042725

First Da Capo Press edition 2009

ISBN 978-0-78672-1009
Published by Da Capo Press
A Member of the Perseus Books Group
www.dacapopress.com

CONTENTS

Sunset Boulevard
William Holden and Gloria Swanson, 1950

Notting Hill
Julia Roberts and Hugh Grant, 1999

INTRODUCTION

In the Beginning,
There Was the Picture

*T*his book began as a collection of fifty profiles, first published in January 2007 in the pages of *Variety*. Our goal then was to ask famous people the question, "What is the movie that changed your life?" We editors purposefully did not include celebrities working in the entertainment business in our project. This collection would be devoted exclusively to "nonpros" (as *Variety* refers to those outside show business). For a young person to see *Citizen Kane* or *Clerks* and be inspired to become a film actor or director is one thing, but what happens when one sees, say, *Rocky* or *Beyond Rangoon* or *Breakfast at Tiffany's,* and is so inspired that he or she decides to become an athlete or an environmentalist or a fashion editor? Since that first collection of profiles, *Variety's* editors have put the question to other celebrities both in and outside Hollywood. At first glance, the question seems overloaded, even preposterous. But *Variety,* the Showbiz Bible, is the kind of place that takes movies very seriously. We depend on them for our livelihood. Surprisingly, as it turns out, so do many others.

Several of the 120 people profiled here answered the question without pause. Some needed a little prodding: "OK, so what is the movie that changed your life *a little?*" Others hesitated, then offered a disclaimer to the effect, "Well, no movie has that kind of power." They invariably went on to describe a movie that had deeply influenced, if not their career, then a personal cause, sociopolitical outlook, or romantic sensibility that would appear to be central to their life. Those examples are as far-flung as Ralph Nader's use of *The China Syndrome* to spark awareness of his anti-nuke crusade and Peggy Noonan's intense identification with the Irish-American characters in *Yankee Doodle Dandy.*

Sometimes the movie's effect on a life's work is even more direct: Candace Bushnell's appreciation of *Annie Hall* led her to cleverly refashion Woody Allen's comedy into *Sex and the City.* Journalists as far-ranging as Tom Brokaw and Lawrence Wright found inspiration in movies as different but apposite as *All the President's Men* and *His Gal Friday.* And among some actors, the link from movie to career is barely a stretch at all: a teenage Jack Nicholson left his New Jersey home and headed to Los Angeles to be an actor after seeing Marlon Brando in *On the Waterfront.* Sarah Jessica Parker saw Woody Allen in *Sleeper* and was hooked for life.

Most of the 120 individuals profiled here see the movies as a powerful medium, one that gets under the skin and goes straight to the soul to shape dreams, aspirations, and attitudes in a way that does change who we are. Certainly the movies change how we see ourselves.

The movies validate. When we don't find characters who immediately reflect our ethnicity, gender, sexual orientation, or cultural upbringing, our instinct might be to reject a movie outright. But often choices proved that idols can transcend these boundaries: Dr. Sanjay Gupta idolized *Rocky*'s very Italian Stallion Sylvester Stallone, while the young African-American model-to-be Tyson Beckford fashioned himself after James Dean in *Rebel Without a Cause.* Elsewhere, the transference carries the viewer across the sexual divide: At age sixteen Ellen Page identified intensely with Jean-Pierre Leaud in *400 Blows;* for Harvey Fierstein, it wasn't a male star he wanted to be but rather Bette Davis, Rosalind Russell, and Barbara Stanwyck in nearly *everything* those actresses ever made.

We all watch the same movie. None of us *sees* the same movie. Take *2001: A Space Odyssey,* the movie most cited in this book of interviews. Authorities and personalities as diverse as Esa-Pekka Salonen, Frank Rich, Dr. Neil deGrasse Tyson, and Larry King all hail Stanley Kubrick's sci-fi masterpiece as one of the most influential movies ever made, and yet each cites a radically different reason why it affected him. Seeing *Gone With the Wind* could hardly have been more different for Civil War historian Doris Kearns Goodwin and right-wing commentator Phyllis Schlafly. Watching *Imitation of Life,* the Rev. Jesse Jackson saw a film about racial identity, while Isaac Mizrahi beheld nothing but "dresses, dresses, dresses."

Liberals in the vein of Howard Dean, Gloria Allred, and Robert F. Kennedy Jr. mention *To Kill a Mockingbird* as a seminal film, citing the character of attorney Atticus Finch as a major influence. Conservatives, in contrast, tend to enjoy heavy doses of celluloid war. Both Sen. John McCain and former speaker of the House Newt Gingrich mention *Sands of Iwo Jima* along with a very long list of other combat fare. Then again, such political opponents as the pro-life McCain and NOW's Kim Gandy both speak of being traumatized as children in the same way by the same film, Disney's animated classic *Bambi.*

Although Disney's fawn feature is deservedly regarded as a classic, many of the movies that have the potential to change lives are truly mediocre, if not downright awful. *Trader Horn, The Wiz, McLintock!, The Mummy,* and *Abbott and Costello Meet Frankenstein* are just a few titles that continue to hold special significance for some of *Variety*'s notables, including such heavy hitters as Gore Vidal and Dr. Leonard Susskind.

Herewith are not the greatest films ever unspooled but rather the most influential, depending on your point of view.

THE ROMANTICS

*"E.T. is about a commitment of taking care of the person you love.
You feel like a better person after watching that film."*
—*Javier Bardem*

Reese Witherspoon *Actress*

She fell in love with Johnny Cash in *Walk the Line* and won her Oscar. But at the movies, Reese Witherspoon only has eyes for another actress.

"I love Natalie Wood! *Splendor in the Grass* is my favorite movie," Witherspoon says of the 1961 romance that has Wood falling madly, passionately in love with Warren Beatty both on-camera and off. "The end of that movie gets me every time," she admits, "the way Natalie Wood comes wearing that white dress and the white gloves and the white hat to the farmhouse at the end of the movie."

Witherspoon is impressed, and frankly, so was the film's director, Elia Kazan, who called the last reel of *Splendor in the Grass* "absolutely perfect," if he said so himself.

Here's the scene that psyched both Kazan and Witherspoon: Natalie Wood's Deanie Loomis, decked out in that aforementioned all-white outfit, comes back to her Kansas hometown after a

Splendor in the Grass
Natalie Wood and Warren Beatty, 1961

few months in a loony bin to see her first love, Bud Stamper—played by Warren Beauty—who is now married to Zohra Lampert, who is pregnant with their second child. For a moment, Natalie holds the couple's mud-stained little son in her all-white arms and realizes that what might have been will never be, because you can't go back, and we hear her trembling but steadfast voice intone the Wordsworth poetry, "Though nothing can bring back the hour / Of splendour in the grass, of glory in the flower / We will grieve not, rather find / Strength in what remains behind."

"Deanie Loomis. Tragic Deanie," whispers Witherspoon, as if she's channeling Wood, who died in a boating mishap off Catalina Island in 1981. Witherspoon then launches into an amazing re-enactment of the scene where Deanie's mom, played by Audrey Christie, asks her daughter if she has "gone too far," and Natalie Wood plunges her entire naked body under the water of the bath-tub and reemerges to scream like a crazy tween, "No, Momma, I've been a good little girl, Momma! I'm a good little, good little, good little girl!"

Witherspoon shakes her head at the memory of Natalie Wood. "Oh, she was so great!"

And then a moment later, Witherspoon jumps to that ab-solutely perfect final reel, and adds poignantly, "And that moment where the wife [Lampert] is in the housecoat and she's pregnant and she looks at the front of her dress, like, 'I'm in a housecoat,' and she's embarrassed. And Bud's out there with Deanie. And they just know they'll never be together, but . . . I don't know. There's something so personal and real about it. Movies don't always have happy endings, and maybe that is a happy ending? It's reality. It's just touching."

Hugh Hefner *Founder-Publisher,* Playboy

He's the man who calls the Hollywood sign "our Eiffel Tower," and spearheaded the drive to save it, and for good reason: *Playboy's* Hugh Hefner credits a repressive Depression-era childhood with pushing him into the much better world of the "drama and fan-tasies" of the movies.

"It was the musicals of Fred Astaire and Ginger Rogers and Alice Faye and Betty Grable and Busby Berkeley that fueled my romantic dreams," says Hefner. And for good reason, he believes. "You could say things in a song that you couldn't say in straight di-alogue," he explains. "There was an escapist wonder to them."

Casablanca
Humphrey Bogart and Ingrid Bergman, 1942

But his favorite music is not from a tuner. It comes when Ingrid Bergman asks Dooley Wilson to sing "As Time Goes By," much to the dismay of Humphrey Bogart, in *Casablanca*. "The film has everything: unrequited love, alienation, patriotism, humor, friendships, and one of the best scripts and scores. It's a real movie movie," says Hefner.

Michael Curtiz's 1942 Oscar winner rates so high with Hefner that he calls every Friday and Saturday night at the *Playboy* mansion "Casablanca Night," and unspools classics from the 1930s and 1940s. "The America that the rest of the world cares about comes from the movies," Hefner believes. "It certainly doesn't come from Washington, D.C. It is an immigrant dream about a quest for personal and political freedom."

On that score, the politically liberal Hefner may not have seen eye to eye with the politically conservative Jimmy Stewart, but he certainly likes Stewart's movies. Hefner lists *Mr. Smith Goes to*

Washington from 1939 as a political favorite; and in case any of his friends missed it over the Christmas holiday on TV, Frank Capra's 1946 follow-up, *It's a Wonderful Life,* also plays often at the Beverly Hills manse.

Despite all his praise of vintage movie fare, the founder of *Playboy* has no time for the censorship that restricted filmmakers during the golden age of Hollywood. Although a wee lad at the time, Hefner vividly recalls the beginning of the dreaded Production Code. "I was coming of age with its arrival in 1934, and saw all the sudden that Tarzan and Jane were dressed more sedately, that Nick and Nora had to sleep in twin beds. I was aware of the censorship and related it to my childhood, because I wasn't getting hugged a lot by my parents. That's the other part of what *Playboy* is about."

If not for the movies, American men may never have experienced airbrushed centerfolds or Vargas illustrations of pretty girls in panties and lace. There's no doubt about it, says Hefner, "There's a direct connection between Busby Berkeley, films like *42nd Street* and *Footlight Parade,* and World War II movie pin-ups and *Playboy.*"

Marilyn Monroe, the magazine's first cover girl, looms large in this universe. "*Some Like It Hot* is her best, she's also very good in *Gentlemen Prefer Blondes* and *Bus Stop,*" opines this M. M. expert.

Fortunately, it's not all old movies all the time at the mansion. In addition to Casablanca Nights, Hefner hosts recent fare as well. "*The Departed* is a movie movie. It moves right along," he says of Martin Scorsese's 2006 Oscar winner starring good cop Leonardo DiCaprio and bad cop Matt Damon. Neil Burger's *The Illusionist,* with Edward Norton's love-struck magician, brought back some old romance to the screen, in Hef's opinion. And the man who launched a hundred Bond girls was very happy to see 007 in shooting form again with *Casino Royale*'s David Craig.

"I like the new Bond," says Hefner. "Ian Fleming used to be a contributor to the magazine, so it's nice to see they're getting back to their roots. Good job."

E.T.: The Extra-Terrestrial
E.T. and Steven Spielberg, 1982

Javier Bardem *Actor*

Watching the movies had nothing to do with Javier Bardem's current job as an actor or even his Academy Award for playing a killing machine in the Coen brothers' 2007 Oscar winner, *No Country for Old Men*. "My whole family comes from acting. It is not something I wanted to be," he says. "I studied painting. Acting is something that found me rather than I found it."

Actually, the actor was born to it. His mother, whom he memorably spoke to in Spanish from the stage of the Kodak Theater during his Oscar acceptance speech, is actress Pilar Bardem, his grandfather is actor Rafael Bardem, and Javier got his first acting gig at age six in *El Picaro (The Scoundrel)*.

An indelible childhood experience at the movies apparently did not include either that early film or any of the other 100 movies his close relatives have made. Instead, the big one is the all-American *E.T.: The Extra-Terrestrial*. Bardem has seen Steven Spielberg's 1982 sci-fi movie more than any other film. "I was eleven and I saw it twenty times. In a row. Like, I saw it at 2 P.M., 4, 6, and 8 P.M. in one day. I felt overwhelmed by the beauty. Even when I see it today, it hits deep in me and always makes me cry," he reveals.

Why?

"Love," says Bardem. "It is such a beautiful love story between this kid and this totally, theoretically dangerous alien. It has to do with trust, with a strong sense of following our instincts and trusting in your love rather than what the other people are trying to tell you to do. *E.T.* is about a commitment of taking care of the person you love. You feel like a better person after watching that film."

Danielle Steel *Novelist*

Despite having sold over half a billion copies of her romance novels, Danielle Fernande Dominique Schuelein-Steel eschews any expertise on the subject of love. "I haven't had a date in so long, I wouldn't know what it is like," says this currently single mother of nine kids. Not that the author of such novels as *To Love Again, Loving, No Greater Love,* and *Toxic Bachelors* doesn't love movies.

Of the classic romances, Steel picks George Cukor's 1940 screen adaptation of Philip Barry's *The Philadelphia Story* for obvious reasons: "I like happy endings. I love Katharine Hepburn. She was the epitome of chic, glamorous and aristocratic; and when they had an auction of her clothes recently, I bought two of her hats." She promptly nailed them onto the wall of her Pacific Heights house, the largest private dwelling in all of San Francisco.

The other Hepburn, Audrey, also strikes a chord with Steel. "I like her looks and her wardrobe, but I didn't like her movies as much," notes the novelist, who grew up in 1950s France and saw few American movies. "I do remember seeing *Lilie* with Leslie

Caron and Mel Ferrer, and I had a big crush on Mel Ferrer, but I don't even remember the story."

Elephant Walk seems to have made a slightly bigger impression. In the 1954 film, Elizabeth Taylor and Peter Finch grow tea and try not to get squashed by the rampaging beasts in British Ceylon. "I was so scared of the elephants, it marked me for life," says Steel.

More recently, the ultra-prolific novelist found special meaning in the Julia Roberts/Hugh Grant 1999 headliner, *Notting Hill*. "I identify with it; she is famous, I am famous," Steel says, referring to Roberts's movie-star character, Anna Scott. "Fame imposes certain burdens on your love life. You have no privacy. Everybody wants to read about the break-up and the divorce. It doesn't afford you any privacy, and people enjoy your disappointment." The following line from Richard Curtis's *Notting Hill* script is especially meaningful for Steel: "Ah, and every time I get my heart broken, the newspapers splash it about as though it's entertainment." Roberts delivers the line with real conviction, and so does Steel.

What the novelist doesn't like are Big Family movies. "No one shows it like it is," opines this expert. An exception is the original *Yours, Mine, and Ours,* released in 1968 and starring Lucille Ball and Henry Fonda. "I didn't enjoy the remake so much," she says of the Rene Russo/Dennis Quaid starrer, which came out in 2005. "I don't like movies that hold big families up to ridicule and make it look like chaos. Steve Martin in *Cheaper by the Dozen,* it infuriated me. There is something wonderful about a big family; it is astonishingly orderly. It is easier to have nine children than two. They don't fight, they help each other. There is an amazing solidarity. They are responsible, and it makes me so angry to see big families so badly portrayed in the movies. It's like a joke tool in the movie, as opposed to portraying what a cool thing large families are."

Nowadays, Steel goes to the movie with her kids or she doesn't go at all. "I won't go alone," she reveals. Not that her in-house movie critics can always be trusted: "My children told me I wouldn't like *Borat,* and I laughed my ass off."

Millie Martini Bratten *Editor in Chief,* Brides

In addition to her *Brides* magazine gig, Millie Martini Bratten serves as editorial director of a dozen other Condé Nast wedding publications that drive this $160 billion a year business. As the foremost arbiter of all that is good and right with weddings, she also has a keen eye for cinematic nuptials.

"I loved *Four Weddings and a Funeral* for its emotional highs and the emotional angst of weddings," says Martini Bratten. "It shows everything that goes on in a wedding. It's all about the catalyst of love."

Mike Newell's 1994 comedy was Hugh Grant's follow-up to *The Remains of the Day* and made the British actor an international star who came to specialize in comedies. The romantic movies that have most influenced Martini Bratten's career at *Brides,* however, are two headlining Grant's erstwhile costar Julia Roberts.

"She was one of the prettiest bridesmaids I'd ever seen, in *My Best Friend's Wedding,*" says the editor. "That gorgeous purple dress she wore. That was before bridesmaids' dresses became fashionable [with that] evening-type look. Julia made them look so good. We saw the styles of bridesmaid dresses change shortly after that film came out in 1997. We got many calls on that dress. It was an example of someone making the dress look very, very good."

Two years later, there was Garry Marshall's *Runaway Bride,* which, in some ways, took a page from Roberts's own off-camera scenario when she canceled her wedding with Kiefer Sutherland, in 1991, to run off with Jason Patric. The actress's couture in that 1999 romantic comedy also rocked the fashion world, says Martini Bratten. "In *Runaway Bride,* Roberts wore some very romantic dresses, such as the off-the-shoulder, fitted bodice, tulle skirt, which she wears in the iconic picture of her on the horse. We still get calls for that dress."

Martini Bratten sees a correlation between Roberts's real-life wedding dress, when she married her second husband, Daniel

Runaway Bride
Joan Cusack and Julia Roberts, 1999

Moder, and her movie-wedding duds: "When she married Moder, the style was also romantic—the halter dress with an embroidered bodice and a shawl over her shoulders. Her hair was swept up with lilies of the valley tucked into her hair. As natural as she is off-screen, Julia's a real glamour girl when she turns it on."

Regarding her own life and career, Martini Bratten is a little less romantic, and she takes special inspiration from a Rosalind Russell classic about a most unique female. From 1958, "*Auntie Mame* is zany and stylish and rule-breaking, and it is great inspiration for going after what you want and grabbing hold of life with gusto," she says. Of course, even the wildly independent Mame Dennis makes it to the altar in the final reel. "What I like so much about weddings is beautiful clothing, wonderful music, and a lot of emotion and romance and style. It's all about a stylish life."

Annie Hall
Woody Allen and Diane Keaton, 1977

Candace Bushnell *Novelist*

The author of *Sex and the City* and *Lipstick Jungle* grew up in a "small town without a movie theater." It was the 1960s, and in an era before DVDs and cable, Candace Bushnell chilled in front of the tube to catch the occasional Three Stooges or Jerry Lewis movie.

"My all-time favorite: *It's a Mad Mad Mad Mad World*," she says of Stanley Kramer's 1963 romp that starred nearly every comic known to vaudeville: Sid Caesar, Milton Berle, Buddy Hackett, you name it. "I still rent [it] occasionally and always laugh out loud at its sheer, unadulterated silliness," says the writer.

Bushnell's own prose straddles the fence between comedy and romance. Merging the two is tough business, she insists. "Picking a romantic comedy is trickier," she adds. But here's her list: *"Bringing*

Up Baby and *The Philadelphia Story* are the gold standards. There's also *The Graduate, When Harry Met Sally, Pretty Woman, Four Weddings and a Funeral,* and *Goodbye, Columbus,* all of which capture the zeitgeist of the uneasy relationship between the sexes in a time when traditional rules may or may not apply. . . . *Goodbye, Columbus* [is] admittedly not considered a great movie, but I love Ali Mac-Graw's imperfect performance and the end with the lovers united."

Then there's Woody Allen's 1977 Oscar winner, *Annie Hall.* Bushnell puts it in its own separate pantheon off in some Eros netherworld: "This is a movie where the lover is not a person but a place, New York City, in which the relationship is not with another, but with the self. *Annie Hall* does beautifully what so many romantic comedies can't: It captures love as it really is, as opposed to how we wish it would be. And makes it OK."

Strange. Did Bushnell just write a review of *Sex and the City?*

She distances herself from giving Woody too much credit for her own success. "In all honesty, I can't think of one particular movie that has changed my life," says Bushnell. "I see movies as accents, points of view, and perspectives that can enrich one's own view of the world. I tend to watch movies for inspiration in storytelling techniques."

2

THE ACTIVISTS

*"My entire career in politics was sparked by
a double feature on a warm August day in Harrisburg."*
—Newt Gingrich

Robert F. Kennedy Jr. *President, Waterkeeper Alliance*

A noted environmentalist lawyer, Robert F. Kennedy Jr. has nothing but praise for Stephen Gaghan's 2005 CIA thriller, *Syriana,* which brought George Clooney an Oscar for supporting actor.

"It's a good environmental movie, even though it doesn't talk much about the environment," says Kennedy. "Instead, it shows how democracy and the environment and energy policy are corrupted by power and money. It's a great illustration of how our values are being corrupted by our dependence on oil."

Not so surprisingly, Kennedy also recommends a couple of hard-hitting documentaries: "Al Gore's *An Inconvenient Truth* [2006] is the most influential film on the environment that has ever been created. It pushed the issue of global warming past the tipping point. And there's *Who Killed the Electric Car?"* he says, pointing to Chris Paine's 2006 exposé of Detroit. "It shows how the auto industry and other powerhouses conspired to destroy much cheaper and cleaner sources of transportation. The film makes the worst kind of conspiracy buffs look rational."

Syriana
George Clooney, 2005

Speaking of big conspiracies, Kennedy takes no prisoners. In 2006, *Rolling Stone* magazine published his article "Was the 2004 Election Stolen?" to which the author effectively delivered a resounding "yes."

If, in fact, any film influenced Kennedy's decision to become an activist lawyer, it was the 1962 screen adaptation of Harper Lee's novel *To Kill a Mockingbird.* In the Robert Mulligan–directed movie, Gregory Peck plays Hollywood's most dedicated attorney ever, and holding the pocket watch of Lee's father in his hand on Oscar night, the actor received an Academy Award for his efforts.

"I was ten or twelve when I saw *To Kill a Mockingbird.* My parents took me," Kennedy recalls. "It was about justice and one person being hard-headed and courageous enough to make America's democracy work."

Howard Dean *Former Chair, Democratic National Committee*

The physician-turned-politician grew up in East Hampton, New York, where his first movie memory was Disney's 1940 animated film *Fantasia,* a box office failure that in its initial release did nothing for the House of Mouse's bottom line. If the movie spooked out Uncle Walt financially, it also had a sobering effect on the future U.S. representative from Vermont. "It's the first movie I ever saw that I remember. While it was entertaining, I remember being frightened by the march of the brooms," Howard Dean says, referring to the "Sorcerer's Apprentice" segment in which Mickey Mouse experiences a housekeeping nightmare.

Better than Mickey was Humphrey Bogart, says Dean. He especially reveres such 1940s classics as *The Treasure of the Sierra Madre* and *Casablanca,* "the one I've seen the most."

Life-altering movies, however, fall strongly in the social-injustice category. "In 1962, I was thirteen years old and I saw *To Kill a Mockingbird,*" Dean recalls. "It was the first movie I had seen about racial injustice. Gregory Peck was extraordinary; so was Mary Badham. The book is very good, but this is one of the few cases where the movie is better than the book. That movie had a great deal to do with my lifelong commitment to social justice."

More recent films touch on Dean's interest in politics, which hasn't abated despite his unsuccessful bid to be the Democrats' 2004 presidential nominee. "I liked *Good Night, and Good Luck,*" he says of George Clooney's McCarthy-era biopic of Edward R. Murrow. "It was like looking at the political process from the point of a view of a news figure."

Dean also appreciates Roger Donaldson's 2000 thriller, *Thirteen Days,* a little-seen Kevin Costner movie about the Cuban Missile Crisis. "I have no inside knowledge about whether it was accurate," says Dean, "but the most interesting part was how it portrays Kennedy backing down the generals who wanted to go to war."

To Kill a Mockingbird
Gregory Peck and Mary Badham, 1962

Gloria Allred *Civil Rights Lawyer*

Gloria Allred grew up going to movies that starred "strong, sassy women" like Joan Crawford, Rosalind Russell, Bette Davis, and Katharine Hepburn. Only later, after going to college and seeing *To Kill a Mockingbird,* did she consider becoming a feminist and a civil rights lawyer.

"I was still in an intellectual cocoon. I was married with a baby; I had my hands full. But that film made its mark on me," she recalls. "I had never known about that kind of racism, and here was this wonderful lawyer, Atticus Finch, who at great risk to himself and against popular opinion defended this unjustly accused black man."

Over the years, Allred has led discrimination suits against the Boy Scouts of America, the Friars Club, and K-Mart, and she represented the Nicole Brown Simpson family during the O. J. Simpson murder trial.

A proud liberal, this lawyer makes it clear: "The impact of motion pictures on young people cannot be underestimated."

With that M.O., she took her grandchildren to see Deepa Mehta's 2005 film, *Water,* "which inspired me," Allred says. "Set in 1938, it's about child brides in India and what happened to them after they became widows. The problem still exists today. Their choices are to kill themselves, marry the younger brother, or live a life of celibacy. It's a moving film and highlights something I never even knew existed."

Richard Gere *Actor*

Richard Gere has been a champion of the Dalai Lama for over two decades, and his espousal of that exiled Tibetan leader's pacifism runs deep. The actor's belief in the positive power of nonviolence took root at the movies.

"I saw *The Longest Day* with my father and I remember it being a wonderful Saturday afternoon," says the star of *Pretty Woman* and *Chicago*. "It was one of those warm experiences that were very special, probably because my dad was there in World War II. I felt some kind of emotional closeness to him that day."

The Darryl F. Zanuck–produced film can be interpreted as a fairly gung-ho World War II movie, but Gere saw nothing but the horrors of combat in its depiction of D-Day on the beaches of Normandy. He credits that perspective to the company he kept back in 1962.

"My dad had a huge influence on me. He's quite an extraordinary, genuinely generous soul," Gere says. "A couple of years ago he gave me this thing I'd written when I was in high school. It was on nonviolence and I'd forgotten it. I read it, and I haven't really changed much at all." To prove it, he points to his chest. "I marched on the Pentagon, and was very proud of a rib that was broken by a U.S. marshal's baton," Gere says, recalling a Vietnam War protest from his youth.

Although the actor's antiwar activism has never dissipated, one film specifically brought it all back in vivid detail: *Witness to War,* Deborah Shaffer's Oscar-winning 1985 documentary about Dr. Charlie Clements, a Vietnam War pilot-turned-doctor. "Clements started treating campesinos [farmworkers] in the Salinas Valley," Gere says. "A lot of his patients there had fingers missing or breasts missing and it turned out most of them were from El Salvador and they had been beaten, tortured, and ravaged by the guards in El Salvador, which were totally supplied and funded by the U.S. I became quite good friends with Charlie, and we traveled all over Central America together. There was certainly a reawakening in me of a sense of responsibility."

Gere received the Hollywood Award for his performance as author Clifford Irving in *The Hoax,* in fall 2007. That same season he watched as his friend the Dalai Lama received the Congressional Gold Medal, which, in the actor's opinion, was the much, much bigger deal. "It's a huge thing," he says. "I've seen a huge difference over the past twenty years of talking about this. Everybody knows who the Dalai Lama is now."

Although Gere says he has no particular interest in making a film about politics, he doesn't rule out playing George W. Bush himself: "If it painted him with all the irony and madness there. Sure."

According to the activist actor, there's politics in almost any film. Take Lasse Hallström's *The Hoax.* "It's the story of how small lies connect to very large lies," Gere says of Irving, who tried to pass off a phony autobiography of Howard Hughes as the real thing. "It connects to presidents who lie and wars that start from lies and obviously how that resonates today." Tellingly, *The Hoax* takes place in the early 1970s, and as Gere says, it "resonates with Nixon, the Vietnam War, and Watergate."

Which brings him to a favorite "political" film.

"I just saw *All the President's Men* again recently," he recalls. "What a terrific film. It really is wonderful. It's so well-played in terms of character, and the storytelling is impeccable. You don't see [many] films like that."

Newt Gingrich *Former Speaker of the House*

"My entire career in politics was sparked by a double feature on a warm August day in Harrisburg," says Newt Gingrich. Indeed, as a kid, this future politician found himself so psyched by one of those movies, *Trader Horn,* set in Africa, that he immediately went to the Harrisburg City Hall to demand that the town build a public zoo. His petition eventually made the front page of the local newspaper, which prompted his army dad, then stationed in Korea, to write back to Mrs. Gingrich to say, "Keep the kid at home!"

Dad's military career greatly influenced his son's choice of movies—"In the beginning, I wanted to be a movie director," says Gingrich—and it helped that the young Newt befriended the local theater owner. "I saw many movies for free. Most memorable was a John Ford trio: *Fort Apache, She Wore a Yellow Ribbon,* and *Rio Grande"*—all cavalry movies, he points out.

"I was an army brat, and the sense of the culture of the army that is captured in those films was stunningly powerful to me," he says. "They instilled a sense of duty and an identity that transcends just taking orders. The army was something you became, not what you did."

While his keen interest in the military never inspired him to enlist or actually serve his country in the army, Gingrich has committed himself to writing (in collaboration with William R. Forstchen) a few novels on the subject, including *Grant Goes East: A Novel of the Civil War.* On that subject, the politician-turned-author counts Edward Zwick's *Glory* (1989) and Ronald F. Maxwell's *Gettysburg* (1993) as two very influential movies.

"There are two strains of intellectual thought that collide," he says of filming or writing about the Civil War. "*The Red Badge of Courage* has to do with thinking of war as horrible, hunting for the cowards and people breaking under the weight of it." And then there's the romantic version, says Gingrich. "There are moments when you have to be willing to die to achieve your goals, and a courageous band of people make the decision that they can make a difference. *Glory* and *Gettysburg* are in that second tradition, which had to do with the emancipation for the African Americans in the Civil War and the nobility of this band of Boston elites who were willing to die for their cause."

Gingrich counts the *Gettysburg* speech that Col. Joshua Lawrence Chamberlain (Jeff Daniels) gives to his Union soldiers as "exemplary of American patriotism at its best. It is an extraordinary example of the spirit that held together the Union Army despite the level of bloodshed."

Of course, the granddaddy of Civil War films exerted its own power on Gingrich, but only in a convoluted sort of way, he believes. Repeated viewings of David O. Selznick's *Gone With the Wind* led him to read Rudy Behlmer's book *Memo from David O. Selznick,* about the autocratic producer's voluminous correspondence with his stars and directors, among them Alfred Hitchcock. As Gingrich tells it, an interviewer once asked the director of *Rebecca* and *Spellbound* what he thought of all those D.O.S. memos. "I have always wondered what was in them," replied Hitch.

The lesson learned? "I can send out memos, but I need to follow them up," says Gingrich.

Religion is often the flip side of war in a political conservative's makeup—or, as Gingrich explains it, "It's the spirit of being willing to die for your beliefs." The Christian martyrs in Mervyn LeRoy's

Gone With the Wind
Vivien Leigh and Clark Gable, 1939

Quo Vadis impress Gingrich as much now as when he first saw the movie as a boy in 1951. "The saints, many of them died joyfully," he says of Deborah Kerr and company.

Gingrich's blessing also goes to William Wyler's 1959 Oscar winner: "*Ben-Hur* is stunningly faithful to the spirit of Lew Wallace, who started out writing a book to disprove Christ and ended up writing a book proving Christ. The end of *Ben-Hur* is as powerful a commitment of faith as anything that has ever been filmed. And Charlton Heston was able to carry it off."

Another Hollywood conservative also performed admirable Christian service, says Gingrich. "Mel Gibson's *The Passion of the Christ* communicates the human side of Christ, and the level of pain involved in the process of the crucifixion was powerfully rendered. It communicated the degree to which God had sacrificed to expiate our sins."

Norma Rae
Sally Field and Gail Strickland, 1979

Ralph Nader *Founder, Public Citizen*

America's Crusader makes two fairly expected picks for his all-time favorite films, as well as one big surprise.

"*The China Syndrome* was the first film on the risk of nuclear-power plants," says Ralph Nader, singling out the 1979 film starring Jane Fonda, Jack Lemmon, and Michael Douglas. James Bridges's film almost replicated reality when Pennsylvania's Three Mile Island nuclear-power plant nearly underwent a meltdown. Lemmon and Douglas stopped during publicity on the movie for fear of exploiting the incident. Nader and Fonda, in contrast, used the crisis to get out the message. "We were in the middle of the antinuclear fight when it came out. It helped us to reach another audience," he notes.

"The same with *Norma Rae* and labor issues," Nader says of the Martin Ritt drama that won Sally Field her first Oscar, in the same year that *The China Syndrome* was released. "Movies extend the message."

That said, Nader doesn't believe that movies influence his own opinions about the big issues of the day. And regarding their impact on his various causes, "There's no way to measure that," he offers. "Everything's a hunch, but the only thing you can say is that it certainly doesn't pull the movement back. Maybe it raises those people's morale who are organizing in an area. Maybe it is a talking point for an organizer with people who aren't very close to the topic. It helps in the sense that you can say to people, 'Have you seen *The China Syndrome?*' when you're trying to explain nuclear power—in that sense it does. It's like an extension of the information flow. But whether you can say a movie changes your life . . ."

According to Nader, message movies come in all varieties, including those that don't wear an issue on their sleeve. Which brings him to his third big choice.

"*Citizen Kane* is just the power of a media mogul," he says. "It's fairly well done."

Kim Gandy *President, National Organization for Women*

"I'm not a big movie person," says Kim Gandy, who heads up NOW.

Considering her memorable childhood moments at the movies, it's easy to see why.

"My earliest recollection of the movies was Bambi's mother being killed," Gandy says of Disney's 1942 animated classic. "I don't know if *Bambi* had any formative effect, but it has stuck with me for forty-five years. I was shocked and sad."

Unfortunately, an even more traumatic movie outing followed her *Bambi* experience, at age nine. Gandy's mother, a true John

Wayne fan, dragged her daughter to see *McLintock!* costarring Maureen O'Hara, in their hometown of Bossier, Louisiana.

"John Wayne spanks her in public!" Gandy recalls of seeing the 1963 Western. The Duke plays a cattle baron who must fight off domestication not only from O'Hara but also from farmers. Even as a young girl from the Deep South, Gandy objected to the film's *Taming of the Shrew* overtones. "I was completely horrified, and I didn't understand why my mother wasn't horrified too," she says. "No one wants to be spanked in front of their friends. That's wrong!"

Back in 1963, only a few feminist groups protested the movie's light handling of domestic violence. "I don't think any of that protest reached Louisiana," says Gandy. "I didn't know of the women's movement until I went to college."

But *McLintock!* undoubtedly planted the seed. "I identified with Maureen O'Hara," says the feminist. "In the old days she's what you'd call 'feisty,' women who had their own identity. Maybe it was my identification with her that made me so upset." Even at age nine Gandy remembers thinking, "I would never have gone back to John Wayne. What's wrong with her?"

Phyllis Schlafly *Founder, Eagle Forum*

The words "rugged individualism" may have gone out of favor with Barry Goldwater's 1964 presidential defeat. No matter. One of his staunchest supporters still finds the term viable, even if, as Phyllis Schlafly puts it, "Modern semantics has tried to diminish it."

The future right-wing author of *A Choice, Not an Echo* saw *Gone With the Wind* in its first run, and calls the 1939 Oscar winner a message movie. "It's the tale of survival," Schlafly claims. "Margaret Mitchell's novel and the movie had an amazing impact on this country. We were just coming out of the Great Depression, and survival was the thing."

Schlafly, who led the fight to defeat the Equal Rights Amendment, also relates strongly to *The Spirit of St. Louis,* the 1957 James Stewart biopic about Charles Lindbergh, which she calls "an incredible story of one man's achievement. It is so different today. The pilots and astronauts have everything done for them. They are riding something that is prepared by a tremendous team. But Lindbergh's was a solo flight."

Schlafly is especially happy that *The Spirit of St. Louis* doesn't muck up Lindbergh's heroic image with any references to his reported pro-Hitler comments delivered on the eve of World War II.

In 2006, Schlafly published the book *The Supremacists: The Tyranny of Judges and How to Stop It,* but finds no inspiration on that front at the Cineplex. "I can't think of any judges in movies I've liked," she notes.

Marion Cotillard *Actress*

Regarding her newfound Hollywood fame, Oscar winner Marion Cotillard recalls a most favorable introduction to the city—or at least its environs. "The last day of shooting *La Vie en rose* was in Malibu on the beach, and we saw a whale and its baby in the ocean. So my first impression of Los Angeles was one of joy," says the staunch Greenpeace activist, who is known to hold meetings in her Paris apartment.

It's doubtful this actress will ever make the big move to Hollywood. "When I first came here, I was a little bit afraid, because I don't drive much. It's an ecological thing," says Cotillard, careful not to pollute except when absolutely necessary. Beyond that, "I love movies. Charlie Chaplin is an inspiration, and this is a city that is almost dedicated to the movies. Why, the streets are even named Constellation and Avenue of the Stars."

When told that Century City's street monikers are, in fact, inspired by the era of the first astronauts, Cotillard laughs off her minor mistake with seasoned French insouciance: "Hey, I just learned something!"

She is, however, dead serious about her work with Greenpeace; it's an activism that runs in the family: "I was born into the movement. My parents are environmentalists, and my grandparents were gardeners."

The movies also played a crucial role in Cotillard's activism. First there is the obvious choice of *An Inconvenient Truth.* "It is interesting and easy to watch and very clear. Cheers to Al Gore!" she applauds.

For Cotillard, however, the pivotal film comes from director John Boorman. "*Beyond Rangoon* is the one that opened my eyes. I was so touched by it that I told myself, I will never be blind to what's happening in the world, and it was the beginning of my activism," she says. Although the 1995 film about the Burmanese dictatorship doesn't deal directly with the environment, its story of a repressive political regime and its effect on the country "shocked" Cotillard into awareness:

"I knew nothing about Burma before I saw this movie about a tourist, Laura Bowman [Patricia Arquette], who loses her passport in Burma and must flee to Thailand. She meets with Aung San Suu Kyi, leader of the National League for Democracy, who fights the military. It was a shock to discover this woman is a hero, and that nobody cared she was imprisoned," says Cotillard.

Dr. Suu Kyi won the Nobel Peace Prize in 1991. "I dream to play Suu Kyi," says Cotillard, who bears a faint resemblance to the Burmese leader. "But it wouldn't be right that a French girl play Suu Kyi."

According to Cotillard, all sociopolitical movements are interrelated. "Everything is connected," she believes. "If you don't take care of the environment, you don't take care of the people."

If her environmentalist parents and the movie *Beyond Rangoon* formed her politically, it was another movie (and her actor parents) that inspired Cotillard to perform.

"A major movie moment from my childhood is John Huston's *Annie*," she says of the Broadway-to-film transfer. The tuner won few critical raves stateside upon its release in 1989, but regardless, Cotillard says she could go on singing "Tomorrow" forever. "My dream is to be in a musical, and I was taken with the singing and tap dancing in *Annie*. As a little girl, I wanted to play Annie. She was my hero. I still love that movie. I'd watch it again."

The positive impressions from *Annie* were reinforced by many repeats of *Singin' in the Rain* on French TV. "On that one, I actually watched it again and again and learned the choreography, and tried to do it in front of the TV," says the actress.

Larry Madin *Director of Research, Woods Hole Oceanographic Institute*

If Steven Spielberg's *Jaws* didn't change his life, it certainly put a crimp in other people's perception of what Larry Madin knows best: fish.

"The movie generated a lot of interest but also fear about sharks," says Madin, an ardent environmentalist. "One thing we've seen in the years since *Jaws* is a reversal of that idea: people now understand that people are far more the enemy of sharks than sharks are of people. For those of us who are in the ocean-science business, we are much more worried about what humans have done to destroy populations of sharks than vice-versa. In later years, even Peter Benchley completely changed his viewpoint there," Madin says of the *Jaws* author.

Madin points out the novelty factor of the 1975 film. "It took a real, live creature and made it the feature in a monster movie. And I don't think that had been done previously," he notes. "It made people really aware of the fact that there are big, ferocious fish in the ocean."

Jaws was shot in the waters around Martha's Vineyard, and it featured a character, Matt Hooper, whom Madin finds very relatable.

"The oceanographer or marine biologist of Richard Dreyfuss's character was not too far off in terms of his characterization," he points out. "Marine biologists are not white-lab-coat kind of people, and they do spend their time on boats doing messy, wet, dirty kinds of things and sometimes they're rough around the edges. So, in a way, it was nice to see that kind of portrayal—it wasn't some buttoned-up scientist stereotype. In fact, we had, at the time, a scientist here named Frank Carey who worked on big fish like sharks and who was very much in that mold. He really looked like an old-salt sea captain. It was nice to see that on the screen."

Although Madin thinks Spielberg's aquatic movie gave sharks a bad rap, its influence hasn't been all negative. "*Jaws* really did elevate the white shark and the big creatures of the sea in people's consciousness. It helped to open up an appreciation of what's going on in the ocean," he says. "The ocean is the biggest thing on the planet for things to live in, and we don't know too much about what's out there."

That said, he offers a stern warning: "The ocean is not so much dangerous for us in terms of being eaten by something, but dangerous in that we're not taking care of the ocean. And the ocean, as a whole, might turn around and bite us if we don't take better care of it."

Gary L. Bauer *President, American Values*

Gary L. Bauer grew up in a working-poor family where his father was an alcoholic and no one had finished high school. "As a child I was always looking for inspiration, something that sent the message that an individual can accomplish something," he says. To that end, the young Bauer found solace in watching two Frank Capra movies on TV.

"I saw *Mr. Smith Goes to Washington* when I was probably in the seventh grade," he recalls, "and it made me begin to think

Mr. Smith Goes to Washington
James Stewart, 1939

about government and politics, and eventually led me to law school and Washington, D.C."

Capra has a lot to answer for. Due to his intense identification with Jimmy Stewart's dedicated but naïve Sen. Jefferson Smith, Bauer founded the political-action group American Values, which advocates against abortion, same-sex marriage, and stem-cell research, and in favor of school vouchers and school prayer, among other issues.

In his early moviegoing days, Bauer also found respite in that same one-man-makes-a-difference message of Capra's 1946 holiday classic, *It's a Wonderful Life*. But a recent viewing on cable TV gave him pause. "You recall the villain Mr. Potter, played by Lionel Barrymore?" he asks. "One of Potter's complaints about George Bailey's Savings & Loan is that they were giving out subprime mortgages to people Potter would never loan money, people who didn't know where their next dime was coming from. It's right out of today's headlines!"

Bauer has a problem with most of today's Hollywood fare, but not all. "Even if they stretch the boundaries of language, I still feel that some movies have a good message in them," he opines. An example is Brett Ratner's 2000 feature, *The Family Man,* starring Nicolas Cage as an unmarried investment broker who wakes up one day to find he has a wife and family. The message, according to Bauer: "The accumulation of wealth becomes more important than the relationship you have with your own children and spouse. *The Family Man* tells us that we're more than our bank account."

Neil G. Giuliano *President, Gay & Lesbian Alliance Against Defamation*

In 1982, years before he was elected mayor of Tempe, Arizona, Neil G. Giuliano went to the movie theater alone, "hoping that I wouldn't run into anyone I knew" in his hometown. The film: Arthur Hiller's *Making Love,* starring Harry Hamlin and Michael Ontkean as lovers. "It was somewhat taboo and embroiled in a media frenzy," he recalls. "I was stunned and even overcome by what I was watching."

Now that he's president of GLAAD, Giuliano finds movies more important than ever "because what people see on the screen changes hearts and minds. That was certainly true for me. Because I was seeing a story about two men in love, who actually kissed, it changed my way of thinking about myself and being gay."

Giuliano saw *Making Love* seven times—"the guy at the ticket counter must have thought I was crazy"—and he so identified with the conflicted (and married) doctor character, Zach, that he bought a sweater vest just like the one Ontkean wore in the movie.

Cut to December 2005: for Giuliano, Ang Lee's *Brokeback Mountain* brought back the phenomenon of *Making Love.* "It was a

Brokeback Mountain
Jake Gyllenhaal and Heath Ledger, 2005

film that made it into the national consciousness. It's just amazing, unfortunate even, that it took twenty-five years for it to happen again in such a powerful and far-reaching way."

Giuliano notes a sea change in audience reaction to the two gay-themed movies. "When I saw *Making Love* in the theater, the audience was quiet," he recalls, thinking back over two decades. "It was not a shocked silence, but rather, the audience seemed to be absorbing the film as it unfolded. It certainly made an impression on me. I remember it played [at] a little theater in a strip mall; it certainly never hit any of the big downtown theaters.

"When I first saw *Brokeback Mountain,* it was in a big theater—a far cry from the theater where I saw *Making Love* twenty-five years before! When Jack and Ennis [Jake Gyllenhaal and Heath Ledger] first got together in the tent, there were literally cheers from the audience, which was made up of men and woman, both gay and straight. It's just a different generation: the gay members of the audience are living openly and honestly, which makes a world of difference in their support of a movie inclusive of gay characters. *Making Love* was made when we were living in the shadows, and the audience reflected that. *Brokeback Mountain* put a loving relationship between two men into the spotlight, and its vocal audience and subsequent accolades show the overall support of the LGBT [lesbian, gay, bisexual, and transgender] community."

Eli Pariser *Executive Director, MoveOn.org*

A key architect behind what the *New York Times* once referred to as possibly "the fastest-growing protest movement in American history," this liberal activist got the calling early on at the Cineplex.

Thinking back to 1989, Eli Pariser says he wasn't much of a "movie-watcher" growing up in rural Maine. "But when I was nine, my mother drove my younger brother and me two hours to the nearest art theater to see Michael Moore's *Roger and Me*. We had no idea what we were going to see—I think the last movie I'd seen was *101 Dalmations*—and both of us probably had bad dreams about the Flint, Michigan, woman who makes her living selling rabbits for food," he recalls. "But it was a formative experience— seeing good working people in Flint suffering the consequences of executives' greed. [It was] a good introduction to the downsides of big business culture, though perhaps a little above my age range at the time."

Pariser also admires *Matewan,* John Sayles's 1987 film about a union uprising in a poor mining community. "It's amazing how little of the union movement's folklore has reached a mass audience, given the profound affect it has had on America," he continues. "As the bumper sticker says, these folks brought us the weekend, but our cultural memory hardly recalls the truly epic struggles men and women went through to get it, putting their lives and their families on the line so that working people could be treated fairly. The savage and violent opposition to these union campaigns is worth remembering, but so is their eventual victory."

Regarding classic film fare, Pariser saw Stanley Kubrick's *Dr. Strangelove* when he was in high school, and it also helped to shape his political bent. "There's a lot to love about that movie— the wicked sense of humor, the outsized characters, and most disconcertingly the sense that nothing that goes down is as far-fetched as it's made out to be. There aren't many better examples on celluloid of what happens when no one takes responsibility for the greater good.

"And that's why I got involved in politics, really," Pariser says, "out of a sense that the powers that be are sometimes asleep at the wheel, or worse, and that unless all of us who are concerned about our greater good speak up, we could face some catastrophic consequences."

Rev. Jesse Jackson *Founder and President, RainbowPUSH Coalition*

"I cried when I saw that movie," Jesse Jackson says of *Imitation of Life*. The 1959 Douglas Sirk sudser helped to resuscitate the career of Lana Turner after her daughter, Cheryl Crane, stabbed and killed boyfriend-mobster Johnny Stompanato. For Jackson, the appeal of *Imitation of Life* has much less to do with Lana, however, than the character played by her costar Susan Kohner, cast as a light-skinned African-American girl trying to pass as white. As Jackson sees it, the movie's racial subplot recalls the story of Esther in the Bible.

"She made some bad decisions," he says of Kohner's character, "but the film showed her inner turmoil and how unresolved her inner conflict is. *Imitation of Life* effectively shows the conflicts of people trying to accommodate themselves into the larger society, and the devastating effects on the mother [Juanita Moore], whom

Lilies of the Field
Sidney Poitier, 1963

this girl denies as her mother. It is so often the oppressed people who internalize the power of the oppressors, their likes and dislikes. She was conflicted and chose her imitated life over that of her own mother."

Working with Martin Luther King Jr. in the 1960s, Jackson especially enjoyed the films of Sidney Poitier, citing his Oscar-winning turn in *Lilies of the Field,* in 1963, as an "interracial breakthrough with great social dynamics and artistic rendering," and likens the actor to such sports greats as Joe Lewis and Jackie Robinson, all of whom "defeated race supremacy," he says. "They were carrying the burden of years of racist propaganda."

Most recently, Jackson took in *Akeelah and the Bee,* which he calls "one of the most meaningful movies I've seen in a long time." Set in South Los Angeles, the story concerns a student [Keke

Palmer] who is mentored by a caring teacher [Laurence Fishburne] and goes on to win a spelling bee. Or as Jackson explains it, "She fights the odds at home, and against those odds somehow emerges as a champion."

In some ways, that character's perseverance is what also impresses Jackson about the real-life careers of Poitier, Robinson, and Lewis: "Whenever a black man overcame those odds to become a champion, he wasn't just the black champion, he was the world champion."

If the movies ever failed to teach Jackson anything, it is in the arena of his life's work. "The parting of the waters in *The Ten Commandments* was exciting," he says of seeing the Cecil B. DeMille classic for the first time in 1956. But did it or any other film ever teach him anything about religion? "No."

Sherry Lansing *CEO, Sherry Lansing Foundation*

Sherry Lansing shattered the Hollywood glass ceiling upon becoming president of 20th Century Fox in 1980, and two years later she upgraded to the CEO slot at Paramount Pictures, a post she held for twelve years. Today, Lansing heads up her own philanthropy, which targets cancer research and education initiatives in the Los Angeles public school system.

"One of the reasons I was drawn to film is that I thought it was the most powerful means of communication," says the former actress turned movie exec. "I thought films could change people's minds and force social legislation." The movies most responsible for shaping her social consciousness, says Lansing, are four classics dealing with anti-Semitism and racism: *Gentleman's Agreement, The Pawnbroker, In the Heat of the Night,* and *To Kill a Mockingbird.*

"And also *Imitation of Life,* even though it's not a masterpiece like the others," she adds. "I saw it when I was nine years old, and I was moved by its theme of racial prejudice. But, hey, all those movies are entertaining. They can't be medicine. But they can be the tipping point of the dialogue."

Lansing also recalls the emotional impact of a lesser-known film, one whose title escapes her memory. "I was in high school or college when I saw it. I remember telling my husband [director William Friedkin] that I have to see it again," she says. "I will never forget its final image: a child is taken away from an interracial couple in the 1960s, and in the last shot the little child is waving goodbye as the car pulls away. I have never forgotten that image, and it is so much more powerful than any dialogue. The film came out around the time of this landmark legislation on interracial marriage, and today there is this landmark legislation on gay marriage, which is the last bastion of civil rights."

Lansing was president of 20th Century Fox when the film company released the gay-themed *Making Love* (see Giuliano profile in this chapter). "We were honored by GLAAD for making that movie," she recalls. "You always hope that people get the social message and that the movie lives on. But again, you have to make it entertaining or no one will come," she adds, illustrating exactly why she managed to stay at Paramount for an unprecedented twelve years.

Regarding Lansing's must-see movie about interracial marriage, it is *One Potato, Two Potato,* a low-budget independent movie directed by Larry Peerce and released in 1964. The film profiles an interracial married couple (Barbara Barrie and Bernie Hamilton) who lose custody of the wife's child when her ex-husband contends in court that a mixed household is an unfit environment for raising children.

THE COMEDIANS

"Little Miss Sunshine inspired me because it showed me that my family was a lot better than I thought. At least our car ran, and my cousin, even at her worst, looks better than Toni Collette."
—*Joan Rivers*

Dave Barry *Author*

Dave Barry points to the "futile and pointless" gesture in *Animal House* as a turning point in his evolution from immature adolescent to immature adult.

"That movie so relentlessly glorifies juvenile guyness," says the Pulitzer Prize–winning humorist. "And I knew that whoever made that movie believed it. It wasn't just a joke. There is no redeeming moment."

The best scene from John Landis's 1978 frat-boy comedy: "There's a big parade in the middle of town, and they completely destroy the parade," Barry notes. "They make this car into this tank and attack the town. A whole, huge, massive genre came out of that movie, and all this 'guy humor' followed it."

Which is what spoils it a bit for Barry with today's *Wedding Crashers*–style movies. "There's always some poignant moment, and in the end they fall in love and settle down." In contrast, *"Animal House* just ends badly, as well it should."

Even though Barry grew up on a TV diet of Three Stooges films, he doesn't count those goons as comic inspiration. "They

Animal House
John Belushi, 1978

were like old guys trying to be funny," he says. "They were trying too hard. Nyuck, nyuck, nyuck. My dad was a huge fan of Robert Benchley and P. G. Wodehouse, so those were more my influences."

For Barry, the second funniest movie on Earth is Norman Jewison's 1966 comedy, *The Russians Are Coming! The Russians Are Coming!,* which showcases Alan Arkin's submarine captain sparring with Jonathan Winter's police captain. "They are brilliant, they are in their prime, and between those two, the movie makes me wet my pants," says Barry.

Arkin provides the evolutionary link to Barry's favorite comedy from recent years, Jonathan Dayton's and Valerie Faris's 2006 feature, *Little Miss Sunshine.* "Arkin's brilliant. I'll watch any movie with Alan Arkin," says the writer. Although he enjoyed

Sunshine from the get-go, Barry had his fears when Arkin's cocaine-addicted grandpa expired halfway through the movie. "I was cringing at what they'd do for the ending," he recalls. "I thought they'd give us a Hollywood ending, and when they didn't, I was so proud of them. The movie remained true to itself to the bitter end."

Steve Carell *Actor*

At no less an occasion than the 2007 Academy Awards, the comedy team of Jack Black, Will Ferrell, and John C. Reilly took jabs at how dramatic actors always hog the honors, leaving their comic brethren empty-handed at the end of the movie-awards season.

Sitting in Hollywood's Kodak Theater that evening, Steve Carell applauded wildly at the trio's routine, and for good reason: in the following month, he would be labeled ShoWest's Comedy Star of the Year, while dramatic actor Don Cheadle was to be honored, quite simply, as Actor of the Year by the theater exhibitors' confab in Las Vegas.

Carell handles his second-class status in typical style—with a joke. "I'm hoping to start with comedies, move toward dramas, and eventually go into pornography," he deadpans. "I'm frankly happy to be employed right now."

In at least one respect, Carell's reference to the sexually explicit plays into Carell's cinematic past, if not his future. "When I was a little kid, my older brothers took me to see my first R-rated film, which was David Lean's *Ryan's Daughter,*" he recalls. "It was the first naked woman's breast I ever saw, and that completely changed my life."

If there's a joke to be made that his first starring role came via *The 40 Year-Old Virgin* and that in his follow-up movie, *Little Miss Sunshine,* he played gay, Carell does not go there. "I just want to do whatever is fun and challenging and, frankly, whatever I get hired to do, and if that something is comedy, then great," he says.

If he says so, then it is great that Carell followed *Virgin* and *Sunshine* with three more comedies: *Evan Almighty, Dan in Real Life,* and *Get Smart,* all made concurrently with his hit TV comedy, *The Office.*

That TV-to-movie redux *Get Smart* is a coming home of sorts. If any film made him want to be a comic, Mel Brooks's *Young Frankenstein* from 1974 is that film, and it is Brooks, together with Buck Henry, who created the original Don Adams TV series.

"As a kid, I saw *Young Frankenstein,* and it holds up, in my opinion. It is just funny," he offers. "I will introduce that film to my children when they're ready to see it. I know they will think that is a funny movie as well."

Sarah Jessica Parker *Actress*

What the *Sex and the City* franchise owes to Woody Allen!

Novelist Candace Bushnell counts *Annie Hall* as an inspiration. And Sarah Jessica Parker saw *Sleeper,* Woody Allen's 1973 sci-fi comedy, at an impressionable age and immediately turned him into a role model.

"We used to go to the movies once a year. And usually we went on New Year's Day," she says of growing up in Nelsonville, Ohio. "One of the first movies I ever saw in my life was *Sleeper.* Woody Allen became iconic to so many of us—an aspirational person in an aspirational city, living this life of an intellectual who was eating interesting foods and talking to interesting people and reading interesting books and being political and being an East Coaster."

Sleeper may seem an odd introduction to the oeuvre of Woody Allen. Its story of a man projected 200 years into a future without sex essentially ended Allen's period of flat-out comedies like *Bananas* and *Play It Again, Sam.* (For *Sleeper,* Allen cast actor Douglas Rain, who memorably provided the voice of HAL in *2001: A Space Odyssey,* to be the voice of an evil computer.) Only two years after

Sleeper
Woody Allen, 1973

Sleeper, Allen made arguably his most famous film, *Annie Hall,* which effectively mixed the laughs with the kind of urban sophistication and angst that impressed Parker in Allen's latter work.

Who knows? Woody Allen may have had something to do with the Parker family's trek eastward to New Jersey and, later, Manhattan, so that Sarah Jessica could pursue a career on Broadway, playing the title role in the musical *Annie*. Allen "was all those things that I strived to be, and my mom and dad were striving to be," says the actress. "I came to know all of Woody Allen's work through that movie."

Parker pretty much devotes her entire pantheon of movie classics to 1970s fare that she knew as a kid and adolescent. In addition to *Sleeper,* seminal films include everything from the children's fantasy *Willy Wonka and the Chocolate Factory* to the surrealistic backstage story *All That Jazz* to the romantic period piece *The Way We Were*. But Parker breaks rank to include one title from 1955.

"Very recently, I saw a film that I cannot get out of my head, and that's *Love Me or Leave Me* about the great singer Ruth Etting and her husband," says Parker. "It stars James Cagney and Doris Day in an absolutely perfect performance. She sings maybe a dozen songs. She's a great interpreter of lyrics and song. So that's kind of my favorite movie right now."

Joan Rivers *Comedienne*

Joan Rivers is all about family when it comes to the movies. Many classics have shaped her life and given her the inspiration to carry on against all odds. For example, *Stella Dallas* and *Mildred Pierce* taught her that kids are always jerks when it comes to their own parents.

"These two movies inspired me when they made me realize that I wasn't alone in having a daughter who was ashamed of me," the comedienne begins. "It was so hard to decide which road to take: Joan Crawford's quiet, drunken dignity or Barbara Stanwyck's flat-out cheapness."

When pushed, she admits that it was probably Crawford, in her 1945 Oscar-winning role as the ultimate suffering mom, who won out. "That line in *Mildred Pierce*: 'You smell of pie!' That is the worst," offers Rivers, thinking back to Ann Blyth's bitch daughter Veda. How could any mother not identify? "But choosing between Crawford and Stanwyck, that was a big choice for me, and I suppose I went for Crawford, who just sits there quietly hiccupping."

Rivers's family riff continues: "*Little Miss Sunshine* inspired me because it showed me that my family was a lot better than I thought. At least our car ran, and my cousin, even at her worst, looks better than Toni Collette."

Did anyone ever mention that Rivers is a little bit fixated on appearances? Good looks versus bad looks is the theme that surfaces regardless ·of the movie mentioned. Here's Joan Rivers's beauty hit list:

"*Frida* inspired me to move to Mexico where you can have facial hair, one eyebrow, and still get fucked. *The Whale Rider* with Keisha Castle-Hughes shows that an ugly little girl who stinks of fish can get nominated for an Academy Award in an ugly dress. This is *soooo* not Jewish. With *Braveheart* I was inspired by the fact that a hairy midget could single-handedly save Scotland. Just think what Dr. Ruth could do for French Canada."

Breaking her comic spiel for a moment, Rivers must digress to criticize the Oscar-winning maker of *Braveheart*. "I found it appalling that they put up a statue in Scotland of William Wallace and it looked just like Mel Gibson!" she cries.

But that lapse of seriousness aside, she is soon back on a roll to mention more ugly people who captured her attention at the movies. "Even though *La Vie en rose* is new, it will serve as inspiration to little girls in generations to come," she believes. "You can whore around, do drugs, drink, and go blind, and you, too, can be a huge star and die alone and crippled at forty-six. Lindsay Lohan had better watch it. And anything with Renée Zellwegger in it: the fact that a girl who in every single one of her movies looks like she just sucked on a raw lemon can be that successful: wow!"

Beauty, or lack thereof, also figures into why *The Bad Seed* continues to strike a real Rivers nerve, especially in light of current California justice, or lack thereof: "This one is inspirational because of the message that it sends," she says of the 1956 child serial-killer epic starring an eleven-year-old Patty McCormack. "You don't have to be a rich celebrity like O. J. Simpson, Robert Blake, or Phil Spector to get away with murder. Sometimes blond pigtails and a snotty attitude can be enough. Talking to you, Britney."

Family, beauty, and then there's décor. Who doesn't fixate on interior decorating when all else fails in a movie?

"*Birdman of Alcatraz* proves that you can take any space and make it pretty and was the inspiration for my country house. I think a cuddle bone really brings a room to life," says Rivers. "And *Citizen Kane* inspired me to finally clean out under my bed and find my old sled."

Jokes aside, Rivers finds nothing funny to say about Federico Fellini's 1954 masterpiece. It was the first film to win the foreign-language film Oscar, and it won over the cynical Rivers as well. "I saw *La Strada* and it knocked me out. It knocked me for a loop," she says. "Because Giulietta Masina plays a clown, I identified with her totally. She is funny and quirky and pathetic. I thought, 'I can do that.' Yes, *La Strada* is the big one."

Art Buchwald *Author*

On the subject of classic movie comedies, Art Buchwald was nothing if not concise. Two weeks before his death in January 2007, the writer revealed to *Variety* the secret behind every successful comedy: "What makes them great are the jokes," he said. And Buchwald was an expert on the subject, having won two Pulitzer Prizes and authored more than thirty books, including his 2006 tome, *Too Soon to Say Goodbye,* about the five months he spent in a hospice. It was a topic that only Buchwald could make funny.

When really, really pushed, the eighty-one-year-old scribe did mention the title of one great film comedy, Billy Wilder's 1959 drag fest, *Some Like It Hot,* but he clearly loathed the thought of singling out any one film for any one reason.

"If it's funny, you laugh," he said. "I sit there and enjoy them, and then I watch something else. I don't have a favorite. I knew those guys who made those films, and I'm admiring of all their stuff."

He was even more emphatic on nixing any thought of how movies might have influenced his own comic sense: "No, I do my own stuff. I do my own thing. That's what I do for a living."

Some Like It Hot
Tony Curtis and Jack Lemmon, 1959

Seth Rogen *Actor-Writer*

Seth Rogen has always had a talent for making people laugh. The only difference now is that the genial redhead generates laughs on a global scale, having scored in everything from *Freaks and Geeks* to *Knocked Up* and *Superbad*.

With his sudden success, the Canadian-born actor has discovered a whole new way of working. "Before, the only reason I got cast in a movie was that I, or someone I knew, wrote [the script] for me to do." Increasingly, other people now do the writing. "*Zack and Miri Make a Porno* is one of the first movies that I've just acted in, and it definitely feels like I'm doing half as much," he says.

In Kevin Smith's 2008 feature, Rogen plays porn entrepreneur Zach and goes the raunch route to make some fast cash. It's an assignment that continues to refine Rogen's current status as the movies' biggest triple-S threat: slacker-stoner-schlub.

Working with Smith is a very big deal for Rogen. "Kevin's movie *Clerks,* when I saw that, was one of the defining moments of my career," he says of Smith's 1994 debut feature. "It's the first movie I saw where the characters were talking like me and my friends talk to each other—about *Star Wars* and blowjobs and what have you. That was tremendously influential in my writing. And then Kevin Smith told me he wrote a movie for me and I'm in. Thank God I really liked it," he says of *Zack and Miri.* It was a very simple process. "Usually you have to put a gun to my head to make me finish a script, and I read *Zack and Miri* in one sitting."

Jamie Masada *Owner-Operator, The Laugh Factory*

Having founded L.A.'s venerable Laugh Factory in 1979, Jamie Masada has watched some of the most luminous comics grace his stage on the Sunset Strip. Yet none of them has equaled the collaborative performance he witnessed as a six-year-old in Tehran: his father and a trio of celluloid nuts.

"The first time I ever saw a movie, it was the Three Stooges," he recalls. "Because I'd been a good boy, my father took my hand, and we walked four or five miles to this store that had a black-and-white TV in the window, and they were showing a Three Stooges movie. We were standing outside and couldn't hear anything, so my father started making up the story."

Masada can't remember the title of the movie, but he recalls everything else in vivid detail: "They were onscreen hitting each other on the head, and my father was explaining, 'Oh, OK, the reason he did that was. . . .' He made up the best story, the funniest story, and I just stood there on the street and laughed and laughed.

The Three Stooges

Then he looked at me and said, 'Making people laugh is a great mitzvah.' And I always remembered that."

Masada left Iran for Los Angeles at age fourteen, alone, determined to break into comedy even though he was broke and could hardly speak English. Through chance encounters and friendships with local comics, he managed to get by and immersed himself in American films, becoming particularly enamored with Woody Allen's *Bananas* and the works of Richard Pryor, whom he remembers quite fondly. When Masada opened the Laugh Factory (just after his twentieth birthday), Pryor was his first headliner; after his set, Pryor declined his cut of the night's meager profits, instead offering Masada $100 to pay his rent.

Despite being at the epicenter of L.A.'s comedy scene for many years, Masada remains a fan and is enthusiastic in his praise for the movies of Jamie Foxx (a Laugh Factory graduate) and Sacha Baron Cohen's breakthrough hit.

"When I saw *Borat,* I was laughing loud, and everyone else was laughing loud, and it just gives me such a high to hear that," he says. "I don't know how else to put it."

Kathy Griffin *Comedienne*

She is arguably best known for very publicly not thanking God or Jesus Christ or the Easter Bunny when she won her much coveted Emmy in 2007. Even those people who never saw her TV show, *My Life on the D-List,* or watched her spar with Barbara Walters on *The View* suddenly knew the name Kathy Griffin. She is liberal and controversial. But life for the Irish-American girl from Oak Park, Illinois, began conservative and Catholic, especially when it came to the movies.

Griffin admits that Stanley Donen's *Seven Brides for Seven Brothers* is a little sexist around the edges, if not right down to its 1954 tuner core. But watching it as a kid, she used to dream, "If only that would happen to me, if only I could be in an arranged marriage. There's a family of guys and they're the same age as this family of girls. What more do you want?"

Otherwise, the movies that changed her life have the distinct beat of a feminist heart. "When I was a down-and-out actress and couldn't get a job, *Working Girl* would come on at two in the morning, and it inspired me," she recalls. "I felt better. But then I never wanted to be Melanie Griffith; she works too hard. I wanted to be Sigourney Weaver, the boss who orders people around. Today, I won't let my assistants watch *Working Girl.* Or *Devil Wears Prada* or *Swimming with Sharks.* Meryl Streep gives Anne Hathaway every opportunity in the world. And in *Sharks,* I don't think it's so bad when Kevin Spacey throws things at his assistant's head. It is a little inappropriate, but it is not illegal."

That Jane Fonda played a New York City hooker in *Klute* never bothered the liberated woman in Griffin, who saw the 1971

Bowling for Columbine
Michael Moore, 2002

film when she was not yet a teenager. "She was smart and taking her acting classes and wearing couture clothes," Griffin says of the Bree Daniels role that landed Fonda her first of two Oscars. It didn't matter that her idol Fonda was having sex for money. "And I was a little too young to get the Hanoi Jane thing," she adds. Much more important, "I saw Jane Fonda at the Academy Awards, and she would say slightly outrageous things. Bette Midler, too. Those girls always stuck out for me. Something outside the grain. So I lobbed them together with Gloria Steinem. I had a whole fantasy world that they had dinner at Bella Abzug's house and Lily Tomlin would come over and make them laugh."

Many years later, Griffin came across a photo of Steinem, Fonda, and Tomlin together, and she almost cried. "It actually happened the way I hoped it did. They were part of something," she says. Now she mourns that loss. "Today it is Paris Hilton and Nicole Richie going to lunch. Not only don't we have Gloria Steinem, we don't have those actresses who do kick-ass roles, get into trouble politically, wear the great outfit, and go with the high-profile guy. Jane Fonda going with Tom Hayden and how it influenced her next movie, *The China Syndrome*—that's what a movie star is."

Michael Moore isn't an actress, but regardless, he's pretty kick-ass and always gets into trouble politically, and he has even been known to say outrageous things at the Oscars. Needless to say, Griffin identifies with the maker of the documentaries *Roger and Me, Fahrenheit 9/11, Bowling for Columbine,* and *Sicko.*

"He really is going against the grain with those movies," she says. "I'm always trying to shout the things that people won't listen to. Which is why I like to offend the Christians, offend any group. That's what Michael Moore does. I can imagine why the guy weighs 400 pounds: the constant death threats and Fox News devoting months of programming to bring him down. I love that."

4

THE FRONT LINERS

*"My brother wasn't like the Tom Cruise character in
Born on the Fourth of July, but I felt his struggle so deeply."*
—*Valerie Plame Wilson*

Sen. John McCain *U.S. Senator, Arizona*

The senior senator from Arizona is a freak, a major popcorn-chomping, ticket-buying movie freak.

John McCain speaks freely about films with the ease and enthusiasm of a lifelong moviegoer, recalling scenes and reciting his best recollections of long bits of dialogue—replete with inflections of the actors' famous voices.

Between criticisms of casting and direction, McCain chuckles over production trivia. "I love the movies," he says. "Cindy and I enjoy going to the movies together. We go quite often." And he and Mrs. McCain take in much more than the usual G-rated pabulum that would go down well with any family-values voter.

Among political films, the senator picks a controversial one. "I enjoyed both versions of *The Manchurian Candidate,* but in the first version Angela Lansbury was just phenomenal," he says, thinking back to John Frankenheimer's 1962 original. "I bet most Americans today probably don't realize that there were thirty-some American prisoners in Korea who decided they wanted to live in China and were not repatriated. By the way, every one of those

The Manchurian Candidate
Angela Lansbury and Laurence Harvey, 1962

came back eventually. America was just shocked that people would decide to live in a Communist country."

McCain finds the premise of Frankenheimer's thriller entirely credible: "It was very plausible at the time perhaps more than now. The phrase 'brainwashing' was coined because of the very extensive indoctrination the Chinese gave American prisoners in Korea, so it was very plausible that they could have brainwashed one, sent him back to the United States, and given him the triggering mechanism. After [President] Kennedy was assassinated, the film was taken off the screens. It's a testimony to how compelling that movie was."

Another top pick for McCain is Robert Rossen's 1949 Oscar winner, *All the King's Men,* starring Broderick Crawford as a southern politician gone mad. "It's a favorite because I think that

Huey Long was a larger-than-life figure in American politics,"
says the senator. "He was one of the real populists in American political history. He was able to galvanize the masses of poor, under-
privileged Americans in a way that very few politicians in history
have. He had these slovenly ways, and he was a caricature of himself, but the fact is, he was one of the most effective and impactful
politicians on the American scene. He scared the hell out of
Franklin Delano Roosevelt."

But the senator's all-time favorite film? "It is a bit political in
its own way: *Viva Zapata!* I'm sure I've seen it four or five times,
but I haven't seen it quite a few years. It was one of Elia Kazan's
least appreciated films. I thought Zapata was a genuine, authentic,
uncorrupted leader who fought to improve the plight of his coun-
trymen. He held true to his principles. There were many terrific
scenes in the movie, but a few stand out."

At this point in his movie monologue, McCain begins to quote
verbatim long stretches of dialogue from the 1952 film, replete
with actor impressions of not only Marlon Brando and Anthony
Quinn but Jean Peters, too.

McCain says *Viva Zapata!* influenced him more than any other
film, "because I had never heard of [Zapata] before I saw the
movie. I became interested in Zapata and started reading about
him. The book that affected me the most was *For Whom the Bell
Tolls,* but, unfortunately, the movie was badly miscast and so it
didn't do justice to the book. Gary Cooper and Ingrid Bergman
were the stars, but the movie didn't click."

As a child, McCain was like most kids and loved all the early
Walt Disney movies, but today he recoils at the thought of the studio's 1942 animated fawn feature, *Bambi*. "I'll never forget the
trauma when Bambi's mother was shot," he says. But moving right
along, he picks a few other winners: "I was always taken with John
Wayne just because of who he was and the people he portrayed.
For example, one of my favorites was *Sands of Iwo Jima*. Most any
movie that Jimmy Stewart was in I always enjoyed, too. I thought

he was one of the really great actors. *Destry Rides Again* was just a fun, great movie."

One fine day in Washington, D.C., McCain actually got to meet the Hollywood great. "Jimmy Stewart was in a room in the Capitol. There was nobody around; I just walked up to him and I said, 'I'm John McCain and I am honored to meet you.' And he said, 'I'm honored to meet you.' It was so touching. It was so much the man—the humility of the guy. We always watch *It's a Wonderful Life* every Christmas. Since they were about three years old, I force my kids to watch it." McCain's favorite scene? "When he's running down the street shouting, 'Merry Christmas.' It's really just a lovely, lovely film."

The senator's favorite actor, however, remains his *Zapata* star: "Of course, Marlon Brando."

As for his favorite actress, "I gotta say Marilyn Monroe. She was one of *the* great actresses in history. If you ever saw *Some Like It Hot,* she was a consummate actress. She has so many great scenes: the scene on the couch where Tony Curtis kisses her and his glasses get steamed up; then there's the scene when they get together in the upper berth," McCain recalls with a laugh. "Jack Lemmon makes these double entendre remarks that are just really hilarious. You got to credit Curtis, too. Joe E. Brown, he was great. There's just one great scene after another."

For anyone who thinks that McCain's movie repertoire is stuck in some Turner Classic Movies rotation, he mentions more current fare. "I enjoyed *Syriana,* although a lot of people didn't," he says, and goes on to give his approval to *The Bourne Supremacy, The Bourne Identity,* and all the *Mission: Impossible* films. "I like those kinds of things, the car chases. Have you seen *The Departed*?" he asks. "It's pretty rough, but I kind of liked it."

Not that this politician is immune to playing the tough critic; he gives thumbs down to one player in the Martin Scorsese Oscar winner. "Nicholson plays too much Nicholson," offers the senior senator from Arizona.

Alfred McCoy *Author*

As an historian of Southeast Asia and what he calls the "covert netherworld," Alfred McCoy makes ample use of documentary films in his classes at the University of Wisconsin–Madison. One film he shows students is Errol Morris's *The Fog of War: Eleven Lessons from the Life of Robert S. McNamara,* which he calls "a brilliant teaching tool."

McCoy explains the significance of that 2003 documentary: "Robert McNamara, though purporting to bare his soul and confess all, is dissimulating by holding up his mentor and former World War II commander, Gen. Curtis LeMay, as a symbol of unrestrained, inhumane bombing—indeed, as an antithesis who, by implication, exculpates McNamara from the taint of such evil."

But like all good films, it contains "the germ of its own critique," says McCoy. "If we turn back to the scenes of McNamara working with LeMay on the mass bombing of Japan's cities at the end of World War II, we realize that McNamara studied at the feet of the master and applied all these lessons learned when he later bombed North Vietnam."

McCoy, who wrote *The Politics of Heroin* and *A Question of Torture: CIA Interrogation, From the Cold War to the War on Terror,* reports that he has never found an espionage film that approached the stunning quality of Carol Reed's 1949 feature, *The Third Man,* set in post–World War II Vienna. That is, until he saw Stephen Gaghan's 2005 tale of CIA intrigue in the board rooms of the American industry and the oil fields of the Middle East.

"For some forty years, it has been a frustrating search until I went to see *Syriana,*" McCoy says. "Apart from a similar tone of moral ambiguity that made *The Third Man* so brilliantly evocative of the Cold War, *Syriana* adds so deft a contemporary geopolitical dimension in its layered plotting that I can only applaud its brilliance."

Evan Thomas *Assistant Managing Editor,* Newsweek

Fond of war films as a kid, Evan Thomas found himself "transfixed as an eighth-grader" with the World War II film *The Enemy Below,* directed by Dick Powell in 1957. Years later, he went on to write the biography *John Paul Jones* and the best-selling war-naval tome *Sea of Thunder: Four Commanders and the Last Great Naval Campaign 1941–1945,* as well as more than a hundred cover stories for *Newsweek,* where Thomas has been assistant managing editor since 1991.

For good reason, he says, "*The Enemy Below* has always stuck in my head. The special effects of those war movies are crude by today's standards, but in the case of that film, they used the human drama: the two captains, Robert Mitchum and Curt Jurgens, captured the incredible loneliness and frightful responsibility of being a naval commander—no one in the world, not the king of England, had more responsibility than a naval commander—and the film pitted them against each other."

Thomas reveals that he actually felt a twinge of kinship with Mitchum and Jurgens when, at age thirteen, he often sailed the Long Island Sound with a crew of one or two on a thirteen-foot Blue Jay.

Whereas *The Enemy Below* enchanted, another naval film from the late 1950s immediately made Thomas's stinko list. "*John Paul Jones* with Robert Stack was one of the real dogs of all time," he says of the John Farrow–helmed film from 1959, with Bette Davis playing her usual queen shtick as Catherine the Great. "I was so excited to see it, and even as a little boy I knew it was no good. It was so tinny and false, and it didn't seem like they were sailing a thirteen-foot boat, much less an eighteenth-century warship."

In addition to *The Enemy Below,* Thomas gives high marks to other war pictures, including *Patton, Das Boot,* and *Saving Private Ryan.* He found only one small detail wrong with Peter Weir's

Flags of Our Fathers
Ryan Phillippe, 2006

2003 high-seas drama, *Master and Commander.* "It's where Russell Crowe hangs from the bow chains," he says. "The last thing a captain would do is hang from the bow chains, because that is where the crew went to the bathroom."

On the war front, Thomas finds a striking similarity between his own *Sea of Thunder* and two World War II films by director Clint Eastwood, *Flags of Our Fathers* and *Letters from Iwo Jima.*

"What I like about Eastwood's movies is that he made a serious and honest attempt to humanize the war—on both sides," says the writer. "During the war, the Japanese and Americans demonized each other as animals and insects. After the war, we tried to glamorize the whole thing. Eastwood is trying to do in his movies what I tried to do in my book—capture the confusion and banality of war as well as the heroism and pathos."

Thomas believes that *Flags of Our Fathers* and *Letters From Iwo Jima* will bring about "an important cultural shift. They really are antiwar movies; they deglamorize war. From *Forrest Gump* through *Saving Private Ryan* and *Black Hawk Down,* Hollywood reflected the popular zeitgeist that was almost nostalgic about war and warriors—that celebrated the Good War and glorified warriors even in wars that didn't go so well (Vietnam, the Battle of Mogadishu). Iraq has taken a bit of the glory out of war and reminded us of how often death in battle is futile."

Eastwood's two movies are different, says Thomas. "They come at a time when Americans are ready to take a more sober look at war, to realize that enemies are human too and that Americans pay a high price even when they survive war."

Kurt Vonnegut *Novelist*

"The message of the film is that war makes people crazy and they behave in bizarre ways," Kurt Vonnegut said of *The Bridge on the River Kwai.* Speaking to *Variety* shortly before his death in 2007, the writer connected deeply with David Lean's 1957 Oscar winner and gave two very personal reasons for his intense identification.

"*The Bridge on the River Kwai* is set only a year earlier than *Slaughterhouse Five,*" Vonnegut said of his own 1969 antiwar classic. "Seeing David Lean's movie was nostalgic in that I was a prisoner of war with the Brits in Germany during World War II, and I was quite familiar with their bravely singing and other ways of maintaining self-respect. I got to like the Brits a lot in Germany."

Taken prisoner during the Battle of the Bulge, Vonnegut found himself locked in a Dresden prison that had formerly been used as a slaughterhouse. Under the Geneva Conventions, cap-

The Bridge on the River Kwai
Alec Guinness, 1957

tured privates could be forced to work for their keep, and when he and his fellow Allies were marched to work every morning, German guards often yelled, "A hundred pigs used to live here. Now you do." Those experiences, along with the firebombing of Dresden, became the inspiration for *Slaughterhouse Five.*

Even without the personal associations, Vonnegut claimed that *The Bridge on the River Kwai* would top his list of war movies. "The movie is a work of art and not the message," he said. "I was as impressed with *The Bridge on the River Kwai* as I was with *All About Eve,* which isn't about war or me at all. Movies are so important; they are so effective. They take charge of you entirely."

Unlike most novelists, Vonnegut spoke favorably of the moviemakers who brought his novels to the screen. "*Slaughterhouse Five* is marvelous," he said of George Roy Hill's 1972 screen adaptation.

"It's better than the book. There are two people who should be eternally grateful to Hollywood: me and Margaret Mitchell."

Valerie Plame Wilson *Former CIA Agent*

Born on the Fourth of July brought it all back for one future spy.

Twenty-one years before Oliver Stone made that seminal Vietnam-vet picture, Valerie Plame was a little girl whose older brother served in the Marine Corps. "It was 1968, and he was wounded in the Tet Offensive," she recalls. "The Marines knocked on our door and we weren't there, and when we returned home a neighbor told us, 'The Marines came to the door.' We knew what that meant. My father asked, 'Is he alive?' It took a couple of weeks, but we found my brother on a hospital ship. He was in and out of V.A. hospitals for a couple of years, and had numerous operations on his arms. He didn't talk about it."

In 1989 Plame Wilson saw the Oliver Stone film and watched as the real-life character, paraplegic Ron Kovic, rebuilt his life after a horrific stay in a V.A. hospital. "My brother wasn't like the Tom Cruise character in *Born on the Fourth of July,* but I felt his struggle so deeply," she says. "It came home to me, not only what my brother had gone through but what all these young boys have seen and lived through, as in any war, and then they try to come back and fit back into society. That's the power of movies: they are so emotional."

Today, Plame Wilson's brother is "well-adjusted with his own family," she says. "But he could have gone in another direction." It's a fact that led Plame Wilson to find special significance in the 1975 Oscar winner starring Jack Nicholson and directed by Milos Forman. *"One Flew Over the Cuckoo's Nest* is also powerful," she says. "It points out how precious mental health is, and how easily you can go back and forth over that line."

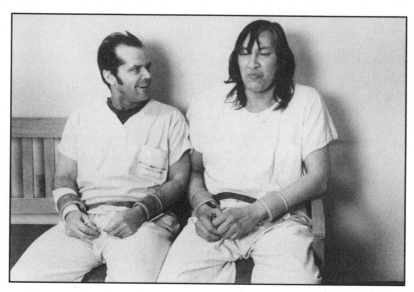

One Flew Over the Cuckoo's Nest
Jack Nicholson and Will Sampson, 1975

Plame Wilson wrote about her experience of being outed as a CIA agent in her 2007 autobiography, *Fair Game*. Regarding the conflicts in the Middle East that impinged her own personal story, she gives high marks to the film version of Mariane Pearl's *A Mighty Heart* and to the actress who portrayed the widow of the slain *Wall Street Journal* reporter. "I forgot it was Angelina Jolie, which is not easy to do, given who she is," says Plame Wilson. "The movie is an accurate portrayal of the chaos in that part of the world, as well as what happens when we are dealing with extremists of any type and how things can spiral out of control so quickly. We need, as a world, to provide an avenue for moderates in every nation to speak out. Extremists come in all different stripes— whether you believe the Book of Revelations should replace the U.S. Constitution or that jihad excuses the killing of innocents— and they are all just as lethal to a healthy human condition."

Lawrence Wright *Author*

Until he saw Peter Greengrass's *United 93* in 2006, Lawrence Wright had found Hollywood lacking on the subject of his book *The Looming Tower: Al Qaeda and the Road to 9/11,* which won the Pulitzer Prize for general nonfiction.

"I'd been discouraged by the failure of the creative community to address what happened on 9/11," he says, "so I was really impressed by *United 93.* The devotion to accuracy and the lack of any kind of hype in that movie—it was played so straight, so honestly. It was a wonderful piece of filmmaking."

Looking back at his career as a journalist, this *New Yorker* scribe finds himself deeply influenced by two very different movies.

"I drew a lot from *The Battle of Algiers,*" Wright says of Gillo Pontecorvo's 1966 film. "As a journalist, that mixture of the real and the imagined really intrigued me. What I do as a journalist runs in that vein, it draws from reality heavily, and then I try to imagine an event that I know. The movie is fascinating in how it used real people, like Brahim Haggiag, in many ways like *United 93.* And in the film there is this figure of the French soldier [Jean Martin], the counterterrorist, who is placed in such a great moral quandary. That was a big inspiration."

Wright also admires a more old-fashioned approach to his job. "Ben Hecht was a hero of mine," he reveals, "and there's the romance of that kind of 1920s Chicago journalism that I never got to practice. I love *The Front Page* [1931] and all its versions, especially *His Girl Friday* [1940]. There's a sense of the adventure and the fun and the ability to dive into life-and-death issues, which is always exciting. That kind of irreverence is still an essential quality in the psychological makeup of the journalist."

Wright enjoyed Bennett Miller's 2005 biopic, *Capote,* and especially praises the acting by Philip Seymour Hoffman and others in the film. But as a journalist, he begs to differ with the film's thesis that Truman Capote unraveled due to moral qualms regarding the reporting of his nonfiction book *In Cold Blood*.

"I've done those kinds of stories myself," he says, "and been placed in those awkward moral situations that reporters find themselves. The truth is most people just stop writing. I'm frightened of that myself. I look at my peers, and many drop by the wayside. At least Capote had the consolation of money and fame; he may have just run out as a writer. His later work wasn't remarkable, and he may have known that. It is a lot of work to write a book, and maybe he didn't have the energy. I'm fighting that now. After working on a long project, it is hard to focus on anything new."

Regarding *In Cold Blood,* Wright doesn't believe, as the Bennett Miller film proposes, that Capote lied to or misled the killers, Perry Smith and Dick Hickock. "He betrayed them in that he imagined their stories," says Wright, who goes on to both approve and disapprove of Capote's methods. "My world is formed by that book; that is, the latitude it suddenly gave to journalism and the invitation to extend your voice into people's minds and their deepest secrets," explains Wright. "But I've practiced that kind of journalism, and I know the difference between what is real and what sounds real and what almost sounds real—and *In Cold Blood* is probably not. In the broad strokes it is accurate. Capote famously didn't take notes. I have total respect for the *New Yorker* fact-checkers, but Capote's subjects were dead. So what did the checkers check?"

When it comes to replicating the reporter's world, Wright gives higher marks to Spike Jonze's 2002 dark comedy, *Adaptation,* which, he says, made him feel "like I was being stalked, like I was being spied on." In the film, the real-life journalist Susan Orlean (Meryl Streep) has her book turned into a script by the real-life screenplay writer Charlie Kaufman (Nicolas Cage). "Those are my worlds, the *New Yorker* and Hollywood," says Wright, who wrote *The Siege* screenplay and is "buddies" with Orlean. "I even stay at the Parker Meridien, where Nic Cage stayed in the movie, when I go into the *New Yorker* office." But "the shock of recognition" went way beyond a few major coincidences. The movie got to the heart of Wright's worst fear: "Every screenwriter experiences it—the difficulty of writing something and then having to condense it for the movies."

Sen. James Webb *U.S. Senator, Virginia*

Before he became a senator, James Webb served with the Fifth Marine Regiment in Vietnam and wrote such best-selling books as *Fields of Fire* and *The Emperor's General*. In other words, he is an expert on war films.

And the films that have influenced him most are the ones that "show leaders facing overwhelming odds, and in the process inspiring others," he says. *Braveheart* is a good example. "So is *Man of La Mancha* in its own way, although the [stage musical] was obviously far more effective than the film. I've always enjoyed those war films that deal more with the emotion and human cost of war, as opposed to those that focus more heavily on action sequences," Webb says, mentioning both *Gallipoli* and *The Bridge on the River Kwai,* which he calls "a masterpiece in terms of showing the obligations of leadership under duress."

The war theme continues with a Bruce Beresford movie from 1980. "My favorite 'issues' movie is actually *Breaker Morant,* which deals with three Australian soldiers who were convicted of murder during the Boer War and then shot by a firing squad. This was a brilliant examination of the ambiguities involved in having to fight a guerrilla war," says the Virginia senator. In his previous career as a lawyer, Webb did extensive pro bono work for veterans. "The film was especially topical when I was representing a young African-American Marine who had been wrongly convicted of

Braveheart
Mel Gibson, 1995

murder in Vietnam," he points out, "and it remains topical in the situations that many of our young men and women face in Iraq."

Webb, who had been U.S. naval secretary, resigned that post in 1988 after refusing to agree to a reduction of the navy's force during congressionally mandated budget cutting. After being elected to the U.S. Senate, from Virginia, in 2006, Webb made headlines with his fiery exchange with one commander in chief: "How's your boy?" asked George W. Bush. "I'd like to get them out of Iraq, Mr. President," replied Webb.

Regarding his latest career move, Webb believes that Michael Ritchie's 1972 feature, *The Candidate,* starring Robert Redford, does a good job of showing "how the best intentions of some people can be overshadowed by the cynicism of the electoral process itself."

5

THE FASHIONISTAS

"Darling invented the wild child/woman look. Julie Christie is winking at
whether she is a girl or a woman—she is playing it both ways."
—*Veronica Webb*

Tim Gunn *Fashion Guru*

What other college dean has made the segue to hosting his own
TV shows? Tim Gunn must be the only one. He followed his long-
held gig at Parson's School of Design with assignments at Bravo's
Project Runway and *Tim Gunn's Style*. He credits the movies with
teaching him a lot about clothes.

Gunn especially admires the Givenchy designs that Audrey
Hepburn wore in *Sabrina* (1954), *Breakfast at Tiffany's* (1961), *Cha-
rade* (1963), and *How to Steal a Million* (1966). Although most critics would call that latter movie one of the actress's weaker efforts,
Gunn sees the caper comedy from another perspective. "At the bar
at the Ritz, with the veil—that's one of the great moments in fashion in the movies," he believes. "The great thing about Givenchy,
he wasn't too snobby to design for films. He realized that it was a
way to do fashion with a capital F and yet not be labeled a costume
designer. Would you call Edith Head a fashion designer? She is a
costume designer."

Gunn is aghast to learn that although Givenchy created Hepburn's *Sabrina* fashions, it was Head who took home the Oscar that

year for designing the clothes worn by Humphrey Bogart, William Holden, and everybody else in the Billy Wilder comedy—and she never even bothered to mention the French designer in her acceptance speech!

"Is that true?" gasps Gunn. Unfortunately, yes.

Despite his unbridled admiration for the French designer, Gunn remains loyal to Hollywood's man, who also needed only one name. "Adrian's designs for *The Women* are from Mars," he says, referring to the Parsons grad circa 1918.

In their way, Hollywood designers like Adrian were at the forefront of American fashion in the 1930s and later, Gunn notes: "Before there really was a Seventh Avenue, a lot of designers went to Hollywood. Hollywood was the place to go; you could have fun with it and be creative. Here in New York City, we had sweatshops, and it wasn't until World War II that America became a fashion force."

While Hollywood has dramatically influenced what men and women wear, the movies have rarely turned their cameras on the fashion industry. *Cover Girl* (1944), starring Rita Hayworth, and *Funny Face* (1957) are notable excursions that Gunn admires. "Who could have been a better Diana Vreeland than Kay Thompson?" Gunn says of the latter film, which stars Audrey Hepburn as a book kook-turned-supermodel.

Forced to choose a fashion-movie best, Gunn picks a Michelangelo Antonioni entry from 1966.

"*Blowup* is an incredible fashion movie, one that is 9.8 on the sexual Richter scale," he says. "It gives a lot of insight into the industry of the times but is still relevant, particularly with regard to the whole photographer-model relationship. It can be so lusty and sex-charged. When David Hemmings is straddling Veruschka, the staccato clicking of the camera is almost like a metronome that speeds up as the lust increases."

Are models and photographers really that charged on the job?

Blowup
David Hemmings and Veruschka, 1966

"With the good ones: yes," says Gunn. "When the photographer is passionate and involved, he gets swept up in it. The model is, 'Whatever you want me to do, I'll do.' It's the power of seduction. I don't know what to compare it to. Forgive me: It's like having sex."

Gunn does not dismiss *The Devil Wears Prada* as a total Hollywood fantasy, despite Stanley Tucci's raid on the stylists' closet, which would get any editor, high or low, fired. On the contrary, "*Prada* is a genuine lens on a certain editorial point of view that the future of fashion rests with the magazines. That editorial world has a lot of mysteries and mythologies; it's like looking at a sphinx. There are myriad fashion magazines, and each has a different point of view. *Vogue* and *Paper* couldn't be more disparate. Yet, they will each hold to that theory that it is all about us."

Gunn feels that *Prada* took only one misstep fashion-wise. "When Meryl Streep wears that oversized fur coat, that was not a great moment. But the exaggeration and the shocking impact was part of David Frankel's direction. It had us talking."

Otherwise, "Patricia Field is a genius," Gunn says of the *Prada* (and *Sex and the City)* stylist. "The way in which the movie sent the message of Anne Hathaway's transformation, it was almost surreal. I'm constantly talking about the messaging of what we wear, how we want people to perceive us. Hathaway didn't have to open her mouth; the clothes did that."

In addition to *The Devil Wears Prada,* the year 2006 produced another design-conscious film, in Gunn's opinion: "*The Queen* was another fashion movie. It was 'Don't let this happen to you!' "

Isaac Mizrahi *Designer*

Whether he's designing for uptown (Bergdorf Goodman) or out of town (Target), Isaac Mizrahi never forgets his humble beginnings, which go back to age eight when he sat in front of the TV set one otherwise dreary afternoon to watch a 1959 weeper from director Douglas Sirk.

"I was a tiny, tiny boy when I saw *Imitation of Life* with Lana Turner," he recalls. "They could not have stuffed more dresses into one movie. Jean Louis did the dresses. I remember loving that movie . . . not even understanding the race content. I just loved looking at it. The colors, the composition, and, of course, the dresses, the dresses, the dresses. It was so incredibly beautiful. But I think my favorite fashion film of all time is *The Women*. Adrian did *The Women*. It's just dress after dress after dress."

How appropriate that Mizrahi should make his theater debut, as a designer, with a 2001 Broadway revival of Clare Booth Luce's all-female comedy in which he had twenty-two actresses take their final collective bow wearing nothing but their underwear or, in this case, Mizrahi's undies.

That dream assignment, however, had its challenges, thanks to the movies.

"I have to say it was very difficult for me to not refer to those clothes," he says of Adrian's original wardrobe for Norma Shearer, Joan Crawford, and Rosalind Russell. "I tried desperately not to refer to those clothes, and they were a big shadow to kind of sidestep around. I had to really, really, really rethink the characters and put them more in New York. That's all I could do. For one thing [the play] is set slightly earlier than the movie. So that helped. For another thing, the Adrian clothes were sort of like a Hollywood version of what New York society women wore, and I was actually doing the actual stuff. I was actually copying dresses from that period—Schiaparelli and Chanel and all that."

Fashion and the movies—Mizrahi can't really choose which is more important. "I've always been obsessed with movies," he says. "Shopping is every bit as theatrical as going to the movies, especially these days. I was an acting major in Performing Arts High School, and I have had as much experience acting and performing as I do designing clothes."

Although not a fashion film, Michael Powell's and Emeric Pressburger's 1948 riff on a tale by Hans Christian Andersen, *The Red Shoes,* speaks to Mizrahi in another, equally personal, way. He identifies completely with the story of a ballerina manipulated by a control-freak impresario.

"Everything in that movie points in one way or another to some aspect of my life—the whole fairy tale that underlines it, about how you sacrifice everything for your work," he remarks. "All the colors in that movie and every single thing about it, every single character is just a very resonant thing. It's a beautiful story and very tragic."

Mizrahi is one of the few designers, alive or dead, to have his life filmed, in *Unzipped.*

The Women
Joan Crawford, Norma Shearer, and Rosalind Russell, 1939

"It was something that happened by accident," he says of the 1999 documentary. "Though I was passionately involved in the making of it, I never expected it to go very far, and then the reaction was huge. I hear over and over again from people working on fashion scripts and related projects that *Unzipped* inspired them, which makes me very proud."

Mizrahi also applauds *The Devil Wears Prada* for being accurate in its depiction of fashion-biz types. "It really managed to capture fashion as a character, the actual fashion world, not a televised made-up version," he says. "If a movie is only about fashion, it's going to be a dreadful bore. Meryl Streep, she can do no wrong. She really wasn't doing Anna Wintour. She was doing something else. For her to try to do Anna would have been wrong," he says of *Vogue*'s editor in chief.

Imitation of Life
Lana Turner and Juanita Moore, 1959

Veronica Webb *Model*

Veronica Webb, supermodel and cohost of *Tim Gunn's Style,* insists that getting the right look is a "tantalizing high-wire act which silently telegraphs where I've come from, where I am at, and where I intend to go."

Runways, TV ads, and magazine covers are one thing. But it is the movies that Webb calls "possibly the most powerful example of how dress can be used to create or change how we wish to see ourselves and others to see us."

The former Revlon spokeswoman is not shy to give examples: "Think of Tony Manero crossing the Brooklyn Bridge in his iconic black-and-white three-piece suit in *Saturday Night Fever,* Julia Roberts in a little black dress and diamond choker in *Pretty Woman,*

Lonette McKee in that red number in *Sparkle,* and of course the ruby slippers from *The Wizard of Oz.*"

Webb has no problem recalling how one film shook her high school world in the 1980s.

"*Blade Runner* took all of the early influences of the punk rock era and rolled that into the costuming of Daryl Hannah," she says of Ridley Scott's sci-fi classic about replicants in search of their maker. "It was an aesthetic that every cool chick was trying to capture at the time. In high school, I was desperate for that look from *Blade Runner*. It personified rebellion and futurism and sex and rock 'n' roll in a whole new way."

And it wasn't just one replicant that this future supermodel wanted to emulate.

"Sean Young's costume took the classic Hollywood star look and gave it a futuristic edge. I would have been really proud to walk around like either one of them," she says. And, "There was this scene with a stripper [Joanna Cassidy], who was wearing that amazing clear plastic raincoat. That coat married 1940s glamour with a sex shop–sex worker street look. It's so influential of what post-modern glam is."

Three 1960s films also figure big in Webb's fashion aesthetic.

In Stanley Donen's *Two For the Road* from 1967, "The clothes had an ultra-modern edge and it was at a time when there were all these new space-age fabrics," she recalls. "There's a scene where Audrey Hepburn is clad in black patent leather. It was all in those incredible lines of the silhouette. There's tough fabric that is rendered in an ultra-feminine way. This look was both her social and emotional armor. But it was still so chic. The lifestyle that she and Albert Finney have is so amazing. They even drive their Mini into a plane. They travel to chateaux and billionaires' homes. It was a birds-eye view of the emerging jet set."

Then there's John Schlesinger's 1965 film, *Darling,* which won Julie Christie an Oscar. Webb claims to have seen it every day for one whole year. "*Darling* invented the wild child/woman look,"

Webb says. "The fabrics were tough, and there was a rhinestone ring that looked like it came out of a gumball machine. Julie Christie is winking at whether she is a girl or a woman—she is playing it both ways. In everything I see in Miu Miu, I see that kind of spirit."

And finally, according to Webb, a call girl from one movie changed the face of fashion: "That sexy slip that Elizabeth Taylor wore in *Butterfield 8,* you still see that today in New York designers who do these slip dresses. Lingerie as outerwear—it all started with *Butterfield 8.*"

Tyson Beckford *Actor-Model*

He has sold a zillion threads for Ralph Lauren, Tommy Hilfiger, and Gucci. His favorite article of clothing: James Dean's red jacket in Nicholas Ray's *Rebel Without a Cause.*

"I watched a lot of old movies when I was a kid, and from the time I was six years old, I said, 'I'm going to have a red jacket like that. I had one too,' says Tyson Beckford. "I don't know where it is now."

Growing up poor in the Bronx, the future host of Bravo's *I Want to Be a Supermodel* identified with Dean's angst-ridden teen whose red jacket came to symbolize a generation's despair. "It's what youth is, not only for that era but today," he says. "Our parents are against us, the cops are against us, the man is against us. People tried to help him, but he felt no one was listening to his story. It was me growing up. And that red jacket, James Dean wore it well, and it said who he was."

Dean died in a car crash a few weeks before *Rebel* hit theaters in autumn 1955. "James Dean loved Porsches and with my love of Porsches, it was weird when I had my accident in '05," says Beckford, who had his own near-death experience on the highway. "I thought, 'Is that the way I'm going out?'" Unlike Dean, who died

Rebel Without a Cause
James Dean, 1955

in his Spider Porsche, Beckford was driving a pickup truck. "But it went as fast as a Porsche," he claims.

Beckford's thing for Dean turned into a thing for Al Pacino when, at age thirteen, he saw Brian De Palma's 1983 Miami drug lord picture, *Scarface* (which is an update of Howard Hawks's 1932 gangster film starring Paul Muni as Tony Camonte). "It had a powerful impact. Wow! I saw a lot of guys like Tony Montana," Beckford says of Pacino's Cuban-born hood. "They existed. I didn't want to be that guy. I admired the power. Not so much the killing and crime, I knew that was wrong—it was more the power, the fact of coming from nothing and being something."

More recently, Beckford responded to the depiction of a similarly hard street life in Fernando Meirelle's 2002 film, *City of God.*

"It made me want to be a filmmaker," he says. "I know neighborhoods in the United States that are similar to that. I want to capture stuff like that."

City of God chronicles the very different life choices of two boys who grow up in Rio de Janeiro's slums, "where the police have no control over these gangs of kids," explains Beckford. "*City of God* made me want to get on the other side of filmmaking. I can be the eyes and ears for these children."

Glenda Bailey *Editor in Chief,* Harper's Bazaar

Designers like Givenchy and Adrian were an inspiration for Glenda Bailey, who grew up in Derbyshire, England, watching old movies on the BBC. She loved how their clothes sent such a strong message regardless of the script or the story line; sometimes, fashion even took on a leading role. As a youngster, Bailey often found herself sketching not the actors but the costumes from films like *Rear Window.*

"I loved the fact that Grace Kelly played the fashion director of *Harper's Bazaar,* and I just adored the fact that she had her negligee in that tiny, little case—so appropriate for a fashion director," says Bailey.

Of course, in Alfred Hitchcock's 1954 masterpiece, Kelly is merely a model who reads *Harper's Bazaar*; she doesn't run the place. But no matter. The future Princess of Monaco looks so stunning in Edith Head's costumes that it activated Bailey's young imagination and caused her to speculate on the motives of the film's leading man, who plays a peeping tom.

"It was charming how Grace Kelly just wanted to attract Jimmy Stewart's attention," Bailey adds. "All I could think was, 'She's looking so beautiful in those gorgeously designed outfits. Why was he looking out of the window in the first place?' He should have been looking at her looking so gorgeous."

Breakfast at Tiffany's
Audrey Hepburn, 1961

More glamorously influential than *Rear Window,* in Bailey's estimation, is Blake Edwards's *Breakfast at Tiffany's,* starring Audrey Hepburn as the quirky call girl named Holly Golightly. In the movie's first shot, a taxi cruises north on an otherwise empty Fifth Avenue (back in the early 1960s, it was a two-way street), and out steps a Givenchy-draped Hepburn, eating a Danish and drinking coffee from a paper cup as she stares into Tiffany's window in dawn's earliest light. Hepburn, who loathed pastries, asked if she could eat an ice cream cone instead, but Edwards insisted on the breakfast food. "Anyone who loves glamour, who loves fashion, can never forget the opening of that movie," offers Bailey.

The 1961 screen adaptation of Truman Capote's novel may or may not have changed Bailey's life, but it did mark at least two major junctures in her career. She recalls her first day in New York as a young fashion student: "I dropped my bags off, and the first place I visited was Tiffany's."

Many years later, when she landed the top job at *Harper's Bazaar,* her staff celebrated Bailey's birthday in a most meaningful way: "I was blindfolded, first thing in the morning, and I got put in a car," she recalls. "I wondered where I was going, only to arrive to have breakfast at Tiffany's. My editorial team had organized it. We had breakfast on the first floor—champagne and pastries. And I was allowed to wear very expensive jewelry."

6

THE DREAMMAKERS

"Certainly, I think there must have been things I ripped off
from Alan Pakula and also Sidney Lumet's film *Network*."
—*George Clooney*

Nicole Kidman *Actress*

Of those Hollywood stars who can command seven or eight figures
a picture, is there any one of them who has committed a darker
oeuvre to celluloid than Nicole Kidman? There are her suicide
portraits from *Fur* (playing Diane Arbus) and *The Hours* (playing
Virginia Woolf), which won her an Oscar in 2002. The afterlife in
both *Birth* and *The Others* is fascinating but not exactly a place
you'd want to visit. Even when she does big-budget remakes, like
The Stepford Wives and *The Invasion,* they are exercises in chronic
paranoia. And in *Margot at the Wedding,* her character is definitely
headed for a severe mental breakdown.

Hearing such downbeat news about her many screen portray-
als, Kidman immediately points to her more upbeat fare. "Fantine
in *Moulin Rouge* isn't dark. She's yummy," she says. "I like to play
yummy, something that is the equivalent of chocolate. And Ada in
Cold Mountain wasn't dark. The movie was dark, but she was a
woman in love. I love playing a woman in love. And the movie I'm
making now, *Australia,* it is just warm. It glows."

The Wizard of Oz
Judy Garland, 1939

Kidman may not always choose to walk on the dark side, but for her life as an actress, that's where it all began—in the shadows. "As a child I was far more interested in the Wicked Witch than Dorothy in *The Wizard of Oz*. That's a film that changed my life," she says without qualification. "I loved the drama of the flying monkeys, and that somehow played into my fears. As a child I was fascinated with the many facets of people's lives. I don't see that as dark. I also try to move towards the light, and with that there are some dark stories. I was Dorothy. I wasn't *into* Dorothy. I'm never attracted to people who are similar to me. I like exploring the psychology of different people." Which leads her, momentarily, to see the very big picture of international relations: "If we did that more as a nation, we'd be more understanding of what brings us to-

Breaking the Waves
Emily Watson, 1996

gether than what separates us, because with that comes some deep flaws and some abominable behavior."

Segueing back to the movies, she remarks on another classic, *Gone With the Wind,* to make her point. "If given the choice between Melanie and Scarlett, every actress wanted to play Scarlett. They didn't want to play Melanie. She was so good."

For Kidman, the movies' influence did not end with 1939. She praises *Breaking the Waves* from 1996, the story of a paraplegic who coaxes his wife into having an affair with another man; it led Kidman to director Lars von Trier. "I was incredibly disturbed by *Breaking the Waves,*" she recalls. "That film taps into the capacity to love, where you get to a point that you actually distort yourself. It's a love that reverberates on some Catholic, almost primal, level. It reached so deep in my psyche, I was supposed to go to a dinner after seeing that movie, but I was sobbing and all I could do was go to bed. That film drew me to work with Lars and the film *Dogville*."

John Waters *Filmmaker*

He is, arguably, best known for giving us Divine (Harris Glen Milstead), the drag queen extraordinaire who headlined such cult classics as *Pink Flamingos, Female Trouble, Polyester, Lust in the Dust,* and *Hairspray,* all of which John Waters helmed.

In the musical redux of *Hairspray,* John Travolta took over for Divine, playing the role of Baltimore hausfrau Edna Turnblad. By 2007 the sight of a man in women's clothes had become so mainstream that parents thought nothing of bringing preschoolers to the movie musical. It was a much different story when Waters's first feature film, *Pink Flamingos,* hit the midnight circuit in 1972. Family newspapers like the *New York Times* refused to publish photographs of Divine with his severely arched eyebrows, corseted 300-pound frame, and bleached-out, shoulder-length hair.

"Up until that time, drag queens all dressed like their mother," Waters recalls.

If Divine wasn't exactly a figment of Waters's imagination, the filmmaker did have one female role model who became a major, if not singular, inspiration.

"There wasn't one movie that changed my life, but when I'm asked that question I usually say *The Wizard of Oz,* because of Margaret Hamilton's performance," says Waters. "She's the only movie star I wanted to be. I'm still jealous of her. I never met her, unfortunately, but I wrote to her and she sent me a T-shirt with her name on it."

Waters loves Hamilton's style, at least the way she appears as the Wicked Witch of the West, a role she never would have essayed if MGM's first choice, Gale Sondergaard, had not refused to wear the now-trademark makeup. "In *The Wizard of Oz*, Margaret Hamilton had this beautiful Comme des Garçon–like gown, and I always wanted green skin," he says. "Now that I'm getting old, I have green skin, and I still wear socks like the dead sister in the film."

Hamilton suffered burns during one take of her fiery exit from Munchkinland, but according to Waters, her pain was well worth the result. "I love dry ice as an entrance," he says. "I've learned from Margaret Hamilton. I always was rooting for the witch in that movie, even as a kid. I always wanted to be the villain in movies. And I've always rooted for those roles in life, and eventually made a career out of that."

Paul Thomas Anderson *Filmmaker*

John Huston often fell asleep to a good cigar and a bottle of Scotch imbibed after a long night of hard gambling.

Paul Thomas Anderson fell asleep to Huston's *The Treasure of the Sierra Madre*—at least while he was directing *There Will Be Blood*. The 2007 film about a California oil baron channels Huston in other ways as well. *Blood*'s Daniel Day-Lewis, playing the lead character Daniel Plainview, delivers a grand impersonation of Huston, and the actor even watched documentaries of the great filmmaker to perfect that portrayal. There's also something of Huston's *Chinatown* character, Noah Cross, in Plainview: water is to Cross what oil is to Plainview.

But for Anderson, *The Treasure of the Sierra Madre* is the movie he most tries to emulate.

"I fell asleep to it. It got into the ground water," he says. "That film means so much to me that I turned Daniel Day-Lewis on to it."

Anderson points out the "obvious similarities" between the two films in terms of the outdoor setting and the relentless pursuit of *something,* whether it be gold or oil. "But that doesn't say enough, because that isn't it exactly. It is the economy with which that story is told," he says of Huston's 1948 film. "But at the same time, it's very meaty. Huston just gives you the steak. There's no sides, there's no mashed potatoes, there's no greens. They just give you the steak, and that was it more than anything—that classic storytelling, that traditional storytelling, which I've always tried to do, but I've never felt like I've succeeded. Maybe my natural instincts don't lead me there. So I was trying to practice that thing, direct and simple."

Jack Nicholson *Actor*

He didn't always want to be an actor, but even as a kid, Jack Nicholson couldn't resist the movies. The one that made all the difference? "Brando in *On the Waterfront,*" says the three-time Oscar winner. "I was an assistant manager in the theater in New Jersey when it played, so I probably saw it twelve or fifteen times. He was the guy of my high school generation."

It helped that Elia Kazan's and Budd Schulberg's story of a failed boxer who stands up to the corrupt union bosses took place in Nicholson's backyard, Hoboken. The starstruck seventeen-year-old saw the movie in 1954, and shortly thereafter he trekked across America to make it big in Hollywood. "One thing I knew is that I wasn't going to imitate Marlon Brando or I wouldn't go anywhere. Some people didn't feel that way," he says.

Brando, a New York–trained stage actor, helped to popularize the acting technique known as The Method. But what worked for him wasn't right for everyone. "It hurt a lot of people," explains Nicholson. Eventually, even Brando gave up the emotionally

On the Waterfront
Rod Steiger and Marlon Brando, 1954

draining technique, complaining that audiences didn't appreciate the extra effort.

Nicholson, whose success as an actor came slowly (he found work acting in B movies for Roger Corman before the 1969 film *Easy Rider* won him his first Oscar nomination), approached the craft differently.

"It's always dodgy to talk about acting, but I'm a member of the Actors Studio. Method acting is whatever works, use it," he says.

On the Waterfront may tower as Nicholson's most influential moviegoing experience, but it's nearly impossible to pick a favorite, he says. "I'm a cinephile. I love a lot of movies: *Cul de sac, Citizen Kane,* and *The Rules of the Game* will always make my list."

A Place in the Sun
Montgomery Clift and Elizabeth Taylor, 1951

Sydney Pollack *Filmmaker-Actor*

If it weren't for *On the Waterfront,* Sydney Pollack might never have met Barbra Streisand, Robert Redford, Dustin Hoffman, and Meryl Streep, much less directed them.

"I had a pipe dream in my late teens about being an actor when I saw Marlon Brando," said the director of *The Way We Were, Tootsie,* and *Out of Africa.* "It just blew me away. I thought, 'Wow! If you could act like that, what a profession it would be.' So I tried, went to New York City, which led me into directing."

And again, it was the actors who most influenced him in that second career as a helmer. "Montgomery Clift and Elizabeth Taylor in *A Place in the Sun,* that love story was just so terribly upsetting when he is in jail and the close-ups of his face and hers," said

Pollack. "Probably without my knowing, it sent me into love stories, which is all I've ever done as a director."

Variety interviewed Pollack when he received the Directors Guild's lifetime achievement award at the Palm Springs Film Festival in January 2007. The director, who died the following year at age seventy-three, called the award an honor "but something of an embarrassment. You can't refuse when your guild asks you to accept."

With *On the Waterfront* and *A Place in the Sun,* Pollack gave his nod to American films, but he remained most enthused about the foreign-language films from the 1950s and early 1960s. "When I was young and beginning a career as a director, I was most influenced by the New Wave films," he recalled, slipping the names of Federico Fellini, Ingmar Bergman, and Michelangelo Antonioni into the nouvelle bag of François Truffaut and Jean-Luc Godard. "Their films were in no way made up of the conventional elements of American narrative suspense. They were not horizontal films. They were all vertical explorations of characters and inner feelings and thoughts."

Pollack specifically cited *Jules et Jim:* "It's relatively plotless; three characters spend time together and then get jealous. It was fascinating."

If some critics now find the films of Antonioni, Fellini, and Bergman in any way pretentious or too literary, Pollack was never one of them, but he admitted, "I haven't seen some of them in years. I don't know if Fellini's *8½* and *La Dolce Vita* hold up. I am personally drawn to the darkness of Bergman. I thought his melancholy was so poetically expressed; I just got the poetry in a film like *Wild Strawberries,* this man looking back at his life and the pathos of a life ending."

Pollack didn't deny that Truffaut and company were heavily influenced by American films: "But they digested them and spit them back at us in a different form."

In turn, he and other Yankee helmers who came up in the late 1960s and early 1970s created a golden age of American cinema.

"The other thing that hit at the same time was the high emotional level of all these youth movements," he recalled. "The gay movement, the feminist movement. It was a wild shaking up of everything, and so filmmakers who were part of that and watching the international cinema gave us *Who's Afraid of Virginia Woolf?, Midnight Cowboy,* and *M*A*S*H.*

Regarding the more recent foreign-language scene, Pollack picked director Krzysztof Kieslowski as a personal favorite, especially his *Three Colors* trilogy from the 1990s. "Who could make a film on equality, one on freedom, and another on fraternity? But he did. His early death was tragic."

Pollack looked back at his own Oscar-helmer history with a certain bemused authority. He won for the 1985 drama *Out of Africa* but not for his classic comedy *Tootsie* three years earlier. The latter film arrived when the Academy had slipped into one of its serious modes and decided instead to honor an inspirational message movie, *Gandhi,* starring Ben Kingsley and directed by Richard Attenborough.

Pollack remembered the year very well. "Both films were released by the same studio, and as a result, Attenborough and I were on the same Columbia Pictures airplane going to all those award shows. I knew I was never going to win any," he said, momentarily forgetting that he was honored by the Golden Globes and the New York Film Critics. Still, he understood the overall critical slight. "The voters like comedies but they don't vote for comedies. I don't know if *Gandhi* has faded. *Tootsie* certainly hasn't. Young kids who were born after *Tootsie* know about *Tootsie.*"

And if they hadn't seen it, Pollack would have been the last to criticize them. "You know, I'm really not film literate," said the man who hosted no fewer than forty-six episodes of "The Essentials" series on Turner Classic Movies. "That's why I did TCM. I thought, 'This will make me do some homework.' I had to sit and watch and make notes so I had something to say about them. A lot of the movies I revisited, but a lot I'd never seen before. When people talk about a shot in a Howard Hawks movie and say, 'He does this and he does that,' I don't know what they're talking about."

Rosario Dawson *Actress*

In March 2007, Rosario Dawson was feted as the supporting actress of the year at the ShoWest convention in Las Vegas. Honors also went to her *Grindhouse* costar Freddy Rodriguez, as well as the film's two directors, Quentin Tarantino and Robert Rodriguez.

In more than one respect, the action picture marked a homecoming of sorts for the actress: while playing a hair-and-makeup artist in Tarantino's *Death Proof* segment of *Grindhouse,* she performed similar rough-and-ready genre duty in Rodriguez's previous release, *Sin City*. Dawson's *Grindhouse* assignment was also a way for the actress to connect with the filmmaker who made the movie that changed her life.

"I hadn't thought about acting when I first got discovered and was in *Kids,*" she recalls, thinking back to Larry Clark's 1995 film about a pack of very sexually active teens. "My dad gave me a copy of *Reservoir Dogs*. I was sixteen at the time, and I ended up watching it five times that week, which would have made any other parent nervous. But my dad realized I was really studying the acting."

Apparently, it did not deter Dawson one iota that Tarantino's 1992 caper movie starring Harvey Keitel, Tim Roth, and Steve Buscemi featured no female actors in sizable roles. Dawson identified with the guys and took it from there:

> Here were a bunch of five guys, all in the same black outfit, in one room together and just being phenomenal. That's always been Quentin's genius. A lot of time he puts these characters that all read a bit the same, they're all jive talkers, and he lets the actors develop the characters. On the page they may sound a little bit the same, but onscreen they differentiate

themselves so strongly you can't imagine anyone else playing those roles. It's amazing to see that so early in his career, and it was the first movie I watched as an actor and said, 'Okay, I think I want to do this.'"

Kirsten Dunst *Actress*

Kirsten Dunst started so young in the business (*The Bonfire of the Vanities, New York Story*) that she can't recall seeing a film before she actually started appearing in them. At thirteen, when she performed press-junket duties for her first big starrer, Neil Jordan's 1994 bloodsucker, *Interview with the Vampire,* the actress already knew the correct tact for tackling the momentous controversy of the day:

What was it like to kiss Brad Pitt?

Dunst, who entered the reporter-filled suite at the Beverly Hills Four Seasons Hotel alone without the aid of a flack or parent, could not have been more the seasoned pro. "Look, I'm only thirteen," she began, "and I don't know why you guys are making such a big deal out of this."

In other words, next question, jerks!

In recent years, Dunst has leavened her noisy, big-budget gigs in the three *Spider Man* movies with a nearly mute turn as the titular heroine in Sofia Coppola's 2006 costumer, *Marie Antoinette*. The actress went way back to Lillian Gish and Louise Brooks for her inspiration on that one.

"*Marie Antoinette* was like a silent film to me," she says. "We didn't have much dialogue. It was a sensorial acting experience. I focused on the way the fabric felt, the cake tasted, the palace smelled. I'd never acted in that way before. It informed my acting, and looking back, it helped me in my acting in *Spider Man 3*. It gave me a different perspective on all the tools I have as an actress."

For an actress who first entered our consciousness playing a child vampire—and took a quick detour with Coppola's *The Virgin Suicides* in 1999—it should not surprise anyone that Dunst's choices for most influential films are a little on the dark side: . *Beetlejuice, Don't Look Now, Edward Scissorhands, Night Porter,* and Roman Polanski's Satan-worshipping *Rosemary's Baby*. "Those films change shape; they mean different things to me at different times in my life," she notes. Most formative, however, is the ultimate kid-as-killer movie.

"I remember I got obsessed with *The Bad Seed* (1956) when I was thirteen or fourteen. I loved that movie," says Dunst. "I wasn't embracing my darkness then. It was just after *Interview with the Vampire*. I hadn't embraced the good darkness. I don't mean the dark darkness. But there's a good darkness, and I embraced it."

Arthur Penn *Filmmaker*

The Berlin Film Festival honored director Arthur Penn in 2007 on the occasion of the fortieth anniversary of his most famous film, *Bonnie and Clyde,* a work that has inspired many filmmakers.

For Penn, the movie that made him want to be a filmmaker was Orson Welles's 1941 masterwork, *Citizen Kane*.

"I was about fourteen when I saw it," says the director:

> I didn't go to many films as a kid because I'd been scared by
> a film when I was young. I have no idea which one it was.
> But I went way down below my seat when I saw it; I was six
> or seven at the time. Then I saw *Citizen Kane,* and it bowled
> me over, because up until then I'd been interested in radio
> dramas and I'd heard Welles's Mercury Players on the radio.
> My goodness! I just got lost in *Citizen Kane,* and I've seen it
> since then numbers of times. I was very intrigued by the

Citizen Kane
Orson Welles, 1941

different camera positions, the different visual approaches to a certain scene. It appealed to some kind of latent sense of the theatrical that I was not aware of. It was the theatricality of it that got to me. It seemed to me like the perfect essence of what I didn't really know about the theater and the movies. Finally, I met Orson quite late in his life and got the chance to tell him how much *Citizen Kane* had meant to me. He was very gracious.

The movies and the theater are closely entwined in Penn's career: he directed live TV in the 1950s, and he enjoyed a Broadway career that began with *Two For the Seesaw* in 1958 and, as recently as 2002, brought Tony Awards to Alan Bates and Frank Langella for their turns in *Fortune's Fool*. In some ways, to see what Penn does on stage is to witness his TV and film work. The three media are leitmotifs woven together, one informing the other. Consider, for example, his movie comedy *Penn & Teller Get Killed*.

"I love their wonderfully clever, bright, and spirited sense of comedy," Penn says of the duo's brand of psychotic magic tricks. In that 1989 film, made over a decade before reality TV overpopulated the tube, Penn Jillette, playing himself, taunts a TV audience to murder him, and then spends the next ninety minutes being stalked. "What intrigued me there," says the director, "is that I have a streak of strong appreciation for vaudeville, which I saw quite a bit of when I was about fourteen, and it was still around. I'd see these wonderful actors who could do that one act for ten years, and they would travel from place to place, three shows a day, with it."

Penn & Teller brings to mind similarly themed material of bu-reaucratic madness from the legendary Broadway show *An Evening with Mike Nichols and Elaine May,* which Penn directed in the 1960–1961 season.

"I learned a lot about comedy from Nichols and May," he says. "They came along at a period when America was restrictive, Eisenhowerish. But they didn't do one-line snapper, Bob Hope jokes. They were talking situations, and it was hilarious because they were skating on the events of that time." In turn, it was a *Play-house 90* episode, "Portrait of a Murderer" starring Tab Hunter, in 1958, that introduced Nichols to Penn's work. Eight years later, Nichols made his movie directorial debut with *Who's Afraid of Virginia Woolf?*

Christopher Hampton *Writer-Director*

In the course of his forty-year writing career, quintuple-threat Christopher Hampton has toiled away as a Tony-winning book writer (*Sunset Boulevard*), Oscar-winning screenwriter (*Dangerous*

Liaisons), playwright, translator, and opera librettist. And back in the 1990s, he also found time to direct the biopic *Carrington* and the film adaptation of Joseph Conrad's *The Secret Agent*.

How does he decide whether a story is more right for stage or film? "It's hard to explain, but I feel it very strongly," he says. "They're two completely different mediums, requiring completely different strategies. It's a matter of instinct, really."

His instinct told him that Ian McEwan's bestseller *Atonement* was a script he had to write: "I really admired the book and lobbied for the job." Like several of his plays, including *Total Eclipse,* "it contemplates the responsibilities and dangers and consolations of being a writer. It's also about the power of guilt and creativity. You never know whether what the child has done is an act of malice or a simple mistake, or a combination of the two. But no matter what, it's marked her life—it's a primal wound that's made her an artist."

Hampton, the youngest scribe ever to premiere a play on London's West End, at the ripe young age of nineteen, earned worldwide acclaim for *Liaisons* on stage and screen. The 1988 movie version "was exactly the film we wanted to make," despite their being in a race to the finish line with Milos Forman's similar-themed *Valmont*. "They gave us the money and said, 'Go make it. Just make sure it gets finished first.'"

Hampton's love of movies and collaboration keeps luring him away from the theater back to a medium offering less control and more danger. "A movie is a gamble," he says. "It's like going into a casino, not knowing whether you're going to be busted and out by the end of the first draft, or steer something through to liking what it looks like, which is such a satisfying thing. You have terrible disappointments, projects you invest in and are devastated when they stumble to a fall, or fall down. The highs and lows are pretty extreme."

On the subject of movie influences, "It comes down to certain directors rather than individual films," he says. "I've always loved Billy Wilder, for example, with his wonderful blend between the ideas, language, humor, and the visuals. I also love Luis Buñuel: it's the remorselessness of him, I expect. And the humor, of course.

"When I direct I always like to pick a film to watch over and over," Hampton reveals. On his 1995 biopic about English painter Dora Carrington, starring Emma Thompson, "I wanted to find a film with a lightness of touch and yet that was a tragedy, and I chose François Truffaut's *Jules et Jim.* I watched that every weekend while we were shooting *Carrington.* On *The Secret Agent* it was Orson Welles's *Touch of Evil,* a concrete example in the same field, which someone else has already attempted."

Ben Affleck *Actor-Filmmaker*

As a virgin director on *Gone Baby Gone,* Ben Affleck took a lesson from one of his first directors, Richard Linklater, who had put him through the paces on the high school drama *Dazed and Confused* in 1993. Like Linklater, "I definitely encouraged the nonprofessional actors to contribute their own dialogue," Affleck says. "When somebody didn't feel comfortable with the script, I'd say, 'How would you say it?'"

Affleck thinks back to a letter that Linklater wrote to his *Dazed and Confused* cast. It read: "I encourage the actors to improvise, because if this is produced entirely as written, then this movie will be a massive underachievement." Ditto *Gone Baby Gone,* Affleck believes: "My entire directorial strategy was about creating an environment where I wanted the actors to be able to succeed as best as they possibly could."

Affleck's first decade as a major Hollywood player has been eventful, if not always consistently good. He shared a screenplay Oscar with his friend Matt Damon for *Good Will Hunting* in 1999, then followed up that success with a string of poorly received acting assignments. Ironically, he got his best review, and a Volpi Cup from the Venice Film Festival, for his performance as grade-B

The Rules of the Game
Jean Renoir, Marcel Dalio, and Nora Gregor, 1939

actor George Reeves of *Superman* fame, in 2006's *Hollywoodland*. And now he's directing.

For that helmer debut, there were certainly easier assignments than *Gone Baby Gone,* which, as a Boston-set crime story, had its recent and illustrious precedents, especially for someone who cites Martin Scorsese and Clint Eastwood as major influences. The fact that *The Departed* and *Mystic River* preceded Affleck's Beantown film did enter his thinking—but not enough for the novice director to drop the project.

"That was really scary, in one way, because how could you ever possibly measure up?" he says. "By the same token, I just convinced myself, 'Okay, we won't measure up to those movies. They will always be Clint Eastwood and Martin Scorsese.' But, we were coming from a different place—the smaller underdog movie."

For a more direct influence than either Scorsese or Eastwood, Affleck points to a French master: "At the end of Jean Renoir's *The Rules of the Game* someone says, 'Everyone has their reasons.'

I stole that for the end of *Gone Baby Gone*. I so love that idea, this notion of all these people rationalizing their behavior. Everyone has a reason, and a high-and-mighty justification for it."

Tim Burton *Filmmaker*

Tim Burton doesn't much like movie musicals. Which did not stop him from directing Stephen Sondheim's *Sweeney Todd,* because "it's my favorite [stage] musical. I saw it in London when it first played there. In fact, I saw it several nights in a row," he recalls.

He was to have directed the movie version in 1996, but then he did a sci-fi spoof, *Mars Attacks!,* instead. When the Sondheim movie project came around again, he took the opportunity to make it with his favorite actor, Johnny Depp, who was now old enough to play the Demon Barber of Fleet Street. This is not to say Burton suddenly turned into an Astaire and Rogers or Kelly and Donen devotee over night.

"Obviously, I'm more of a horror movie fan. And in fact, my *Sweeney Todd* is like a silent movie with music, like an old horror movie. I'm just so used to it," he says.

Burton can't pick his favorite horror movie. "*Frankenstein* is very strong in my memory. All the old Universal films [*Dracula, The Old Dark House*] were probably the earliest memories I have of the movies. It's a collective thing. When Johnny and I were talking about *Sweeney Todd,* we used a lot of different references. You can't name any one movie, but you go back to all the horror movies with Boris Karloff, Bela Lugosi, Peter Lorre, Lon Chaney."

The silent movie star of a thousand faces loomed largest of them all perhaps. "It was interesting to have the music on the set every day," he says of filming the Sondheim musical. It was like "making an old silent movie, playing the piano on the set, and the actors really enjoyed it. Their actions are affected, and Johnny really enjoyed that silent-movie style of acting."

When pushed, Burton does cough up one movie musical that, at the very least, intrigued him. "I do remember liking *Guys and Dolls,*" he recalls. "In that one, they don't burst into song. There's a design in the language that fits together with the music, and they work together. I don't think that's the case with a lot of musicals."

In the case of that 1955 production, which pairs Marlon Brando's Sky Masterson with Frank Sinatra's Nathan Detroit, producer Samuel Goldwyn always regretted that he didn't dub Brando's vocals for the Frank Loesser score. (Obviously, he liked Sinatra's performance.)

Burton, for his part, stands behind the casting of Johnny Depp and everybody else in his *Sweeney Todd,* few of whom are professionally trained as singers. "When they talk and then sing, it is not two different things," says the director.

Robert Downey Jr. *Actor*

Robert Downey Sr. is the director who gave the 1960s counterculture such seminal down-with-the-Man movies as *Chafed Elbows* (about the broken welfare system) and *Putney Swope* (in which a black man takes over a top Madison Avenue ad agency). The latter film's poster, which superimposes a black model over a raised middle finger, became classic 1960s wallpaper in college dorm rooms everywhere.

Because he was only four years old at the time, Robert Downey Jr. can't remember a world without *Putney Swope*. To say it changed his life is an understatement. It *was* his life. "My dad was always outside the fray," he says. "He has always been a bit of a weirdo." That outré status worked to Downey Jr.'s favor when, in 1970, he made his film debut playing a puppy in Downey Sr.'s canine comedy, *Pound*.

Going to the movies with Dad also qualified as a trip. "My dad took me to see everything—probably illegally," Downey Jr. recalls.

"They were R-rated, and he just kind of walks in and goes, 'Relax.' It's no secret that my Dad is a film snob, so oftentimes I'd get all excited, get the popcorn, and we'd go in and the credits would role and the opening frame would be mediocre and we'd walk out. And I'd be like, 'But didn't we just get here?' and he's like, 'Trust me, kid. This ain't going to go right.' I'd be like, 'Wow! I guess he knows.'"

And then Downey Sr. took his son to see Philippe de Broca's 1966 antiwar classic, *King of Hearts,* about a soldier (Alan Bates) who is mistaken for an explosives expert. "We sat there," Downey Jr. says, "and the opening credits rolled, and we were almost through Act I and we hadn't left yet, and I kind of kept looking at him and he was observing and watching and seemed to be enjoying it and [was] engrossed. So I would kind of look at him and look back at the screen and then take it in. I felt that without saying a word he was telling me, 'This is the kind of movie we'll stay for.'"

If it's true that liberals beget conservatives, and vice versa, then it's easy to see why Downey Jr.'s early taste in films is strictly mainstream—but with a slight twist.

"*Bad News Bears* is about a bunch of weirdos winning, and I really got off on that," he says of the 1976 kiddie sports film. "Nobody even really liked each other until the end of the movie. I liked it because the weirdos win."

In life, that isn't always the case.

"I am just really grateful that I was born into a family that put its art first," he says. "The downside is that when you put your art first it doesn't always pan out so well."

Downey Sr. did not go on to have a long, commercially fruitful career in Hollywood. And his son's filmwork has been bumpy from a B.O. standpoint—until recently. Having headlined such big-budget extravaganzas in 2008 as *Iron Man* and *Tropic Thunder,* Downey Jr. is proud of his current popular appeal in Hollywood. "Wow! It's just so nice to be in the game," he says.

When he landed *Iron Man* ("I did fight for this part"), it prompted a celebratory phone call to Dad, which ended up with the elder Downey exclaiming, "God, the last time I heard you this excited was when you were screen-tested for *Chaplin*." That 1992 film won Downey Jr. an Oscar nomination.

Playing a superhero in *Iron Man* fulfills an old fantasy, one Downey Jr. enjoyed until he was about eight years old. "But it was beaten out of me," he reveals. "And then I turned forty-two and I'm finally doing this movie."

Not that he has gone so big-budget that he can't remember his indie roots. A favorite recent movie is *Little Miss Sunshine*. "When I see that dysfunctional family, demonstrating to us how we can all be OK," he says, "I kind of feel like it's a triumph for weirdos."

Michael Arndt *Writer*

While *Little Miss Sunshine* has been embraced as a smart road comedy, it's intriguing to speculate how moviegoers might see the film in forty years' time. Will it grow ever more lighthearted? Or will its story of a near-bankrupt family be viewed as emblematic of America's rapidly disappearing middle class in the early twenty-first century?

If so, that economic take is purely intentional on the part of its first-time screenwriter, Michael Arndt, who won an Oscar for his effort.

"It's about a family of limited means, which you don't see in American movies every day," he says. "You never see people talk about money in movies. There are great wardrobes and great apartments. One of the reasons people are able to relate to the family in *Little Miss Sunshine* is that there's that sense of financial anxiety. It speaks to the current moment, this sense of the rich getting richer and the poor getting poorer, and the middle class is torn between these diverging poles."

Arndt, however, resists turning *Sunshine* into *The Grapes of Wrath* of the new millennium. Yes, both the Joads and the

Hoovers set out for California only to encounter financial hardships, hollow dreams, car troubles, and a dead grandparent onboard. "Within the genre of road movies, there are a number of set pieces," he confesses.

But come on—what about that name Hoover, as in deadbeat Depression-era President Herbert Hoover?

"For five years they were the Harveys," Arndt says of the van-rambling family in his long-gestating script. Then, two weeks before filming, rights-clearance problems emerged. "I probably made a list of thirty alternate names; they were able to clear the name Hoover," the scribe reveals. "Because it's a story of economic insecurity, people are able to make connections that are beyond the imagination of the pea-brain writer."

Although he saw John Ford's 1941 classic in high school, Arndt says much more direct influences were Greg Mottola's *The Daytrippers* from 1996 and Isao Takahata's animated *My Neighbors the Yamadas* from 1999, which taught him that "you could make a full, satisfying story about any family."

When he first sat down to write the *Sunshine* script, Arndt feared he would come up with only sixty pages. "I thought it was too small a story, it was just an ordinary story. Then I saw *My Neighbors the Yamadas,* about a Japanese family. It is entirely episodic. It was so charming, so generously humane towards characters. It made me realize that any family had a future film in them."

In his own family, Arndt fondly recalls going to see Mel Brooks's *Blazing Saddles* with his brothers and father, who told the brood, "Kids, I'm taking you to see a movie."

"So we all went over my mom's protests," says Arndt. "It was such a pleasure to listen to my dad laugh. The film has this great ending where they are run out of the studio gates. There is a sense of freedom and anarchy that just made normal life seem very small by comparison."

The memory stayed with Arndt, who in turn took his own children to practically every Mel Brooks and Woody Allen movie ever released. "Making people laugh is this valuable thing to do with one's life," he says. "It isn't trivial. I saw how much pleasure these movies gave my dad." And Mom's protestations aside, Arndt knows in his heart, "When you're young, it's the fart jokes you talk about."

When it comes to great writing, however, this writer picks the 1982 drag comedy *Tootsie* as "the most perfect screenplay," he claims. "I don't mind that *Gandhi* won the Oscar for best picture: it is big and important and historic and epic. But the fact that the screenplay Oscar went to *Gandhi* and not *Tootsie,* to me it will always feel like an injustice."

Regarding his own Oscar-winning script, Arndt says that *Sunshine* "couldn't be more of an ordinary, straight-ahead linear narrative," because, as a first-time screenwriter, "I was trying to write as low-budget a script as I could."

Nothing wrong there. "Ozu and Fellini started writing light comedies and then made the transition to more serious films," he points out. "My next couple of films will be straight-ahead comedies."

After that, watch out! "I have an idea for a sci-fi film that would be like *Blade Runner* and *Apocalypse Now* set five hundred years in the future as directed by Kar Wai Wong," he says. "There will be time-jumps and fragment scenes and hopefully a formally innovative film that would be a lot about memory."

Edward Zwick *Filmmaker*

Edward Zwick made his name in TV and film with iconic contempo dramedies like *thirtysomething* and *About Last Night,* only to switch to a much larger canvas at the end of the 1980s with his Civil War epic, *Glory.* Since then, he remains fascinated with the big picture, not to mention big-name stars, whether it be *Legends of the Fall* with Brad Pitt (1994), *The Last Samurai* with Tom Cruise (2003), or *Blood Diamond* with Leonard DiCaprio (2006).

"I've been interested in what is epic in very personal stories and what is personal in epic stories," he says. "I'm not sure they are mutually exclusive."

Blood Diamond, set in 1995 during the Sierra Leone civil war, focuses on forced labor camps and the recruitment of children by rebel armies. Despite that powerful story, Zwick doesn't call it a message movie. "The film has to work in terms of a personal story, which must be its most passionate focus," he says. "That's why people go to the movies. You invest in relationships and the journeys of characters. The politics, as such, resonate outward."

One plotline in *Blood Diamond* retells a famous story from the Old West: a man attempts to recapture his lost child, who has become assimilated into an alien culture. In John Ford's *The Searchers,* it is the Native Americans who do the kidnapping; in Zwick's radical update, it's the rebel armies of Sierra Leone.

"*The Searchers* is an enormous influence," says the director. And not just in its story line. Ford's stylistic flourishes also inspired Zwick: "When I was filming *Legends of the Fall,* I found myself framing images through the doorway, and had to stop myself. What am I doing here?"

If Zwick and his *Blood Diamond* screenwriter, Charles Leavitt, borrowed a bit of plot, they did not use Ford's Western to coax a performance out of Djimon Hounsou, who plays the searching father in their film (and received an Oscar nomination for his efforts). In fact, Zwick never revealed his source material to his Benin-born actor.

"As a kid I watched a lot of John Wayne movies," says Hounsou, "but I don't know *The Searchers.*"

George Clooney *Actor-Filmmaker*

George Clooney made his directorial debut with *Confessions of a Dangerous Mind* in 2002, and three years later he followed that

Network
Faye Dunaway, 1976

story of a TV producer-turned-CIA hit man with an even scarier story (because it's true) about the TV journalist who broke the McCarthy blacklist in the 1950s: *Good Night, and Good Luck,* starring David Strathairn as Edward R. Murrow.

Despite his Hollywood base, Clooney remains most fascinated by Washington, D.C. "I grew up in an era when films were reflecting a lot of political upheaval," he says. "I was particularly interested in a good kind of reporter movie, the best of which was probably *All the President's Men.* I liked the newsroom atmosphere, in that I thought they did that really well. Certainly, I think there must have been things I ripped off from Alan Pakula and also Sidney Lumet's film *Network.*"

Fear of exposure permeates Clooney's *Good Night, and Good Luck,* just as it does Pakula's famous trilogy of paranoia, which links *All the President's Men* to the director's earlier efforts *Klute,* in which Donald Sutherland's detective prevents Jane Fonda's prostitute from being murdered, and *The Parallax View,* in which Warren Beatty's reporter uncovers a vast right-wing political conspiracy.

To create fear in an audience, it's best to activate at least one phobia. Clooney, beset with budgetary restraints, came up with the perfect solution for his Murrow biopic. "We wanted to get across this idea of claustrophobia because we knew that our budget [$7.5 million] on *Good Night, and Good Luck* was such that we were going to have to keep the action inside the newsroom," he says. "In some way, that made it easier to create tension. In that respect, I thought about films that Lumet had made earlier in his career, like *Fail-Safe* and *12 Angry Men,* where you don't really travel outside of a bubble."

Ellen Page *Actress*

Ellen Page has been acting on camera since she was ten years old, and with films like *Hard Candy* and *Juno* to her credit, she has already established a reputation for excelling at characters who carry around a moral burden of worldliness despite their few years. The same could be said of the fifteen-year-old Jean-Pierre Leaud when he essayed the lead in *The 400 Blows,* the nouvelle vague touchstone of youthful alienation. Page counts François Truffaut's 1959 film debut as the movie that most inspired her.

"When I first watched it, I felt like I was watching *all* of my favorite movies, because the film had clearly influenced so many people," she says. "I remember watching it, and inexplicably feeling so much watching this boy go through what he goes through. It's usually when I'm inexplicably made to feel so much, even though *The 400 Blows* is so still and so quiet, that I get excited. When any art form makes me feel anything that profound, it makes me feel passionate not just in the sense of being an actor but also passionate in the sense of being a human being."

Page, who was sixteen when she first saw the Truffaut film, identified strongly with Leaud, who "was just a kid, not an actor." She even studied footage of Leaud's early auditions for Truffaut, which she calls "particularly profound."

Hal Ashby's *Harold and Maude* and Lynne Ramsay's *Ratcatcher* are other films that made a big impression on Page. "I like approaching [films] by being as nonanalytical as possible, and, first and foremost, soaking my heart in it. And as cheesy as that sounds, connecting my heart to someone else's," she says. "To me, that's what always feels the most profound, when I watch a film and it just goes straight to my heart. If it doesn't, I actually sometimes have trouble watching the film."

Salma Hayek *Actress-Producer*

George W. Bush had a problem answering "choice or necessity" when it came to his biggest quest. But not so Salma Hayek. "It's a choice," she says of producing Latino-themed movies and TV shows. "But the things we choose are what we also need."

The actress-producer is quick to point out that most projects simmering at her production company, Ventanarosa, are not pegged to her own onscreen ambitions. Still, it's impossible to imagine the Frida Kahlo biopic *Frida,* which made Hayek the first Latino actor ever to be Oscar-nominated as lead player, would have gotten made otherwise. Ditto TV's *Ugly Betty,* which Hayek exec-produces and lent her star glamour to in its opening weeks.

"I produce because I want to create more opportunities out there for Latinos and women, and because I can also do it. So why not?" she says, and then adds, "I love/hate it!"

The love part is obvious. As for the hate, Hayek lists the usual frustrations: "It takes such a long time, and there are so many

Willy Wonka and the Chocolate Factory
Gene Wilder, 1971

people involved. You're as weak as your weakest links." But in the end, "I have a head for it."

To the general public who knows Hayek as an actress, it may seem odd to dwell on her producing career, but that's the way she sees it when she talks about the movies that changed her life.

"With both of them, it was a love for films that I found," she says. "It wasn't the acting. The acting came easiest to me at the time. I didn't have the courage to know that I wanted to produce."

If she had been born a few generations earlier, Hayek would love to have produced Giuseppe Tornatore's 1988 Oscar winner, *Cinema Paradiso,* and the original 1971 version of Roald Dahl's *Willy Wonka and the Chocolate Factory,* with Gene Wilder playing the whacked-out confectionist.

Both films take Hayek back to her childhood in Coatzacoalcos, Mexico: "I was very little when I saw *Willy Wonka* and because of it, for the first time ever, I realized there really is a place where we can make anything happen. You can have a river of chocolate. It's a place with no limits. You can let your imagination go and escape. You don't have to settle for what life has given you, as wonderful as it is. You can explore things that even defy the laws of nature and physics."

Later, when as a college student in Mexico City she saw *Cinema Paradiso,* its story of a filmmaker's childhood friendship with the local projectionist "reminded me of my little town. It really reminded me of myself as a little girl. Yes, with both *Cinema Paradiso* and *Willy Wonka,* it was the love for films. It wasn't acting."

THE BLOODHOUNDS

"The cop in me loves L.A. Confidential.
That movie doesn't slow down no matter what happens."
—Joseph Wambaugh

James Patterson *Novelist*

You can read his film reviews on jamespatterson.com, and they're not exactly love letters despite his admission of being "loony" about the movies.

"It drives me crazy how Hollywood is killing the thriller," says James Patterson, best-selling author of the *Alex Cross* and *Maximum Ride* mystery series. "They do these dreary, very political thrillers that keep tanking, like *Rendition*."

And he has a thing about crime thrillers, like *Gone Baby Gone,* that repeat the ultimate cliché: "I don't want to see another cop movie with a funeral unless there's a reason for it. In publishing, we call it plagiarism. In the movies, they call it homage."

Gone are the days, in Patterson's opinion, of such great suspense pictures of the 1970s and 1980s as *The French Connection, The Marathon Man,* and *Fatal Attraction,* and though his list also includes Lawrence Kasdan's *Body Heat*—the film that made Kathleen Turner a star, in 1981—he isn't so sure about that film's obvious inspiration, Billy Wilder's 1944 murder yarn, *Double Indemnity,* with

Barbara Stanwyck doing her best Lady Macbeth routine. "I'm not sure I've seen that movie," says Patterson. "I'm not into the older movies, from the 1930s and 1940s."

Fortunately for him, his "movieholic" days began in the 1950s when he attended movie theaters that sported gloriously popcorn names like the Broadway, the Ritz, and the Academy, which introduced him to top-drawer Alfred Hitchcock fare like *Rear Window, North by Northwest, Vertigo,* and, of course, *Psycho* from 1960. "It scared the hell out of me," Patterson recalls. "I went with my girlfriend, we were seventeen, and we were afraid to get into the car after seeing *Psycho.* Hitchcock has the power of shock, surprise, suspense, and the twist."

Working on his TV series *Women's Murder Club,* Patterson tried to emulate what he learned from the master. "I always want more twists in the plot," he says. "Hitchcock was also stylistically wonderful. It is the difference between movies and the theater. Everything in Hitchcock is kind of stagy, and he wanted it that way."

And Hitch knew how to tell a story economically. "Every scene should be designed to move both action and character forward," Patterson insists, whether it be a novel or a film. Hitchcock achieved that, and so did William Friedkin with his 1971 Oscar winner, *The French Connection.* "There's that scene where Gene Hackman as the cop is outside the restaurant freezing his ass off, and inside Fernando Rey, the drug lord, is having a great dinner. That's great," says Patterson. "I also love the detail, like that stupid hat Hackman wore."

But clicking on jamespatterson.com, it's clear that this crime writer is not excited by hard-ass detective work alone. "I'm a big weeper. I'm such a girl sometimes," he admits. "I like Jane Austen. Period." And that includes the movie adaptations *Sense and Sensibility, Pride and Prejudice,* and *The Jane Austen Book Club.* "Although now I'm getting sick of her," says Patterson. "Jane Austen was mine. Now she's everybody's."

Psycho
Anthony Perkins, 1960

The French Connection
Gene Hackman, 1971

Michael Connelly *Novelist*

Robert Altman's *The Long Goodbye* led Michael Connelly to his current address on High Tower Drive in Hollywood. He had seen the 1973 update of the famous detective novel when he was in college, and it turned him on to Raymond Chandler. "It's all tied together, and that film means a lot to me," says the best-selling author of *Blood Work* and *Echo Park*, which finds Harry Bosch back in action.

After toiling as a low-paid copy editor at the *Los Angeles Times*, Connelly enjoyed some success as a writer, making it possible to rent the very same High Tower Drive apartment that Elliott Gould's Philip Marlowe kept in the 1973 noir. "Altman filmed it there, and the [cigarette] match scratches are still on the bedroom wall," he says. Out of respect, Connelly and previous tenants didn't dare paint over the evidence. (The exterior of that Milano Kay–designed apartment complex also makes an appearance in Kenneth Branagh's 1991 movie, *Dead Again*.)

If Connelly retains a "sentimental attachment" to *The Long Goodbye,* he calls *Chinatown* his absolute favorite detective film: "It is steeped in the myth of Los Angeles and the fix: Jake Gittes [Jack Nicholson] is the last guy to know what's going on. Noah Cross [John Huston] pulls all the strings. And that would be 'the fix' to me."

In his novel *Echo Park*, Connelly gives a "nod to *Chinatown*," he reveals. "The mystery of *Echo Park* is there at the end. Same with *Chinatown*. You never get to Chinatown until the last ten minutes of the film."

Connelly has no complaints for what Hollywood did to his serial-killer yarn *Blood Work*, which Clint Eastwood headlined and directed in 2002. "Clint Eastwood was twenty-five years older than the guy in the book, but it was fun. He did a good job of capturing the character," says the scribe, who remains philosophical on the subject of movie adaptations: "If you take their money, it's their turn to tell the story."

Chinatown
John Huston and Jack Nicholson, 1974

Crime-wise, Connelly also likes what he sees with more current movie fare: "In *The Departed,* I liked the struggle between the good and the bad, and the undercover cop who's in both camps."

Mark Fuhrman *Author*

After having found the bloody glove that linked O. J. Simpson to the murder of Nicole Brown Simpson, detective Mark Fuhrman found notoriety and lost his job with the Los Angeles Police Department. If he had it all to do over again, "I never would have answered the damned phone at 1:05 A.M. on July 12. I wasn't even on call," Fuhrman says. Now hosting a radio talk show out of Spokane, Washington, the ex-detective says he'd return to cop work "in the snap of a finger." In fact, he became an author with the best-selling *Murder in Brentwood* in order to answer his critics.

Bullitt
Steve McQueen, 1968

"I probably wouldn't have written it if they hadn't indicted me. It kind of ruffled my feathers," Fuhrman says.

Still, he has nothing but admiration for his old profession, especially as embodied in the iconography of Steve McQueen. Fuhrman calls himself an unabashed "trivia hound" on the subject of the blond tough guy. "I don't think McQueen said thirty words in any movie, but he had this ability with his face and body to convey so much that never needed to be said. I'm not sure if his film *Bullitt* specifically pointed me to law enforcement," says Fuhrman, but nonetheless it is a favorite film. "McQueen is the king of cool. In *Bullitt,* his job and his case trumped everything in his life. That is a level of integrity that's in short supply."

Right up there with Peter Yates's 1968 cop movie, in Fuhrman's opinion, is McQueen's penultimate movie, *Tom Horn,* released in 1980, the year the actor died of lung cancer. "I was already a cop by then, but it influenced me. I've watched *Tom Horn* more than a dozen times," he says.

Fuhrman calls McQueen's real-life character in the film "one of those transitional Western heroes, from the nineteenth to the twentieth century. They couldn't eliminate rustling, and when Tom Horn did it, they couldn't turn him off. They had to frame him for the murder of a boy, and by doing so they hanged him."

The trial in Wyoming in 1930 was "a big deal," says Fuhrman, who takes particular relish in Horn's refusal ever to tell his prosecutors whether or not he actually killed the boy. "There's so much of Tom Horn that I've seen in so many people in the police department, that level of integrity where you only care about those people who understand what you're about and where you're going."

Dominick Dunne *Author*

The late 1950s were pivotal for Dominick Dunne, a writer who has spilled much ink on the trials of O. J. Simpson, Robert Blake, and Phil Spector. And for good reason.

In 1958, "I lived right around the corner in Beverly Hills from Lana Turner," he recalls. "On the night of the Johnny Stompanato stabbing, I heard the sounds of the police and was out the door. I stood outside Lana Turner's house and watched as Jerry Geisler, the criminal lawyer, went in and out. My wife was ashamed that I was standing there agog on the street. That was one of the stories that most influenced me."

The other was the Leopold and Loeb murder case as fictionalized in the 1959 film *Compulsion,* starring Dean Stockwell and Bradford Dillman as two college students who, with premeditation and without motive, kill a fourteen-year-old Chicago boy. After seeing the Richard Fleischer film, Dunne promised himself, "Someday I'm going to write like that. Number one, the film truly shocked me. And two, it fascinated me."

Dunne admits to being obsessed by crime stories, but not just any old crime story. "The people all have to be rich!" he insists.

It also helps if the stories are set in Hollywood. Although no one gets bumped off in *The Bad and the Beautiful,* Dunne calls the 1952 Vincente Minnelli film arguably the best movie about the movies ever made. "It is right on the fucking nose!" he declares. "It captures the complexity and the duplicity of the industry. Kirk Douglas and Lana Turner are brilliant."

Prior to his writing career, Dunne produced a few movies, including *The Boys in the Band* (1970) and *The Panic in Needle Park* (1971), and knows firsthand that you don't have to be murdered to end up with a dead career in Hollywood. "I've seen both ends of it, and the horrible part is worse than the successful part is good. It's a fascinating place."

Neither murder nor Hollywood, however, figures into the movie that really changed Dunne's life. "I must have been twelve, thirteen when I saw Bette Davis in *Now, Voyager*. I saw it five days in a row," he says, thinking back to the 1942 weeper. Davis's character, the introverted Charlotte Vale, turns her life around when she finally stands up to her domineering mother, played by an especially chilly Gladys Cooper. "I was so unhappy because of the abuse I took from my father. That film showed me that it was possible to totally change your life, as Bette Davis did in that movie," says Dunne.

As an adolescent, Dunne responded viscerally to the film's Cinderella story, which vividly chronicles the overnight transformation of the homely Charlotte into the beautiful Charlotte. "It made such an impression when she walks off that boat—I can still see it," he says. "She is this new person, and I thought, 'That could be me!'"

Joseph Wambaugh *Novelist*

As a former cop and current author, screenwriter, and college professor, Joseph Wambaugh has a very special L.A. crime movie for every hat he wears.

"The novelist in me has always loved *Double Indemnity,*" he says. "The dialogue sparkles, the plotting is superb. The movie is so good that one can forgive Barbara Stanwyck's horrible blond wig.

"The screenwriter in me loves *Sunset Boulevard,* because it shows how we screenwriters get screwed by studio bosses. I love that theme.

"The cop in me loves *L.A. Confidential.* It comes from an author I like, James Ellroy, and the film has an energy and pace that I seldom see. Pace is something that's hard to teach. You have to feel pace, whether you're writing a novel or a screenplay. That movie doesn't slow down no matter what's happening.

"And I tell my students at UCSD to emulate *Chinatown,* which has a classic three-act structure."

The author of *The Choirboys* and *The New Centurions* doesn't hesitate to reveal why Los Angeles has it over New York, Chicago, and Miami when it comes to writing about crime or showing it in the movies. "I can tell you that in one word: 'Hollywood,' " he says. "Hollywood is always there, somehow, some way. It's no accident that when I went back to write a novel after twenty-some years, I went to Hollywood," he says of his 2006 book, *Hollywood Station*. "Hollywood is the heart of L.A. Hollywood is the heart of the LAPD."

Wambaugh is happy to report that murder Hollywood-style is alive and well at the Cineplex. "Obviously, I'm fascinated with Hollywood and movies, so I did like *Hollywoodland,*" he says. "Ben Affleck's performance was pretty damned good."

Regarding movies that actually changed his life, Wambaugh mentions two.

"Before I began writing, I read John le Carré's *The Spy Who Came in From the Cold* and then saw the movie," he says, referring to the 1965 Cold War thriller directed by Martin Ritt and starring Richard Burton.

> When I began my closet career as a writer, I didn't tell anyone, not even my police partner, and that was the movie and book that kept coming back to me. Le Carré wasn't so interested in how the spy did his job but how the job affected the spy. The emotional trauma suffered by the protagonist was so much more interesting than the run-of-the-mill spy thrillers and gadgetry and James Bond stuff that were so red-hot at that time. That was spoof stuff. When I began writing, I easily changed a few things around from the novel and movie and saw *The Spy Who Came in From the Cold* as a police story. *That* had an influence.

On a more personal level, Blake Edwards's *Days of Wine and Roses,* starring Jack Lemmon and Lee Remick, deeply affected Wambaugh. "As a young cop, my partner and I went to see *Days of Wine and Roses* at the Wiltern Theater on Wilshire Boulevard," he recalls, thinking back to 1961. "I go to the restroom, where there was a lot of gay activity. We get a call to catch some guys, but I want to watch the movie." Wambaugh and his partner then proceeded to fight with a restroom arrestee who ultimately "goes purple" in the brawl. "At first I thought I killed the guy," and so Wambaugh gave him mouth-to-mouth resuscitation.

"I had to see the end of the movie some other time," Wambaugh says. But when he did, it was worth the wait. "*Days of Wine and Roses* inspired me to quit smoking—when I saw the hell that Jack Lemmon went through to quit drinking. I also quit going to the Wiltern Theater, either on-duty or off-duty, after that night."

THE ARTISTES

"With *All About Eve,* Mankiewicz succeeds in creating a screenplay
that is both a delightful caricature and an absolute truthful
portrait of the types that exist in our business."
—*Michael Tilson Thomas*

Plácido Domingo *Tenor-Conductor-Impresario*

In recent years, Plácido Domingo has continued to sing and conduct operas around the world while also overseeing his twin responsibilities as general director of the Washington National
Opera and the L.A. Opera.

As Domingo tells it, he might have done none of those things if
not for MGM.

"The three musicals which made the greatest impact on me
were *The Great Caruso, Singin' in the Rain,* and *Seven Brides for Seven
Brothers,"* says the tenor-turned-conductor-turned-impresario.

> The impact of Mario Lanza's voice on me was enormous and
> helped to crystallize many things in my mind—most impor-
> tant, that being an opera singer could be a very fulfilling ca-
> reer. To this day, I haven't figured out whom I have to thank
> most for that revelation: Caruso or Lanza. However, one
> thing has always been clear to me: that nature had given
> Lanza a phenomenal voice which was highly underrated by

the classical music establishment. I think I can say with confidence that he was too talented by nature and too lucky as a movie personality to be seriously appreciated by the music cognoscenti—for reasons I do not fathom even to this day. Tales abound that he was temperamental and undisciplined. Maybe so, but that should not deflect from the truth that Lanza's voice was an inspiration not only to me but to countless other opera singers, as time has proven.

Indeed, Domingo wasn't the only one of the celebrated Three Tenors who adored Lanza's movie legacy. Luciano Pavarotti cited him as an inspiration, and José Carreras once said, "If I'm an opera singer, it's thanks to Mario Lanza."

But it's also true that Lanza (born Alfredo Arnold Cocozza in Philadelphia) proved to be an undisciplined talent and suffered a short, difficult life in the wake of his enormous Hollywood success. After *The Great Caruso* became the top-grossing film in the world in 1951, Lanza's temper and weight problems got him into trouble on a follow-up project, *The Student Prince,* in 1954, and MGM fired him. Ready to resume his aborted opera career, he died in Italy in 1959. He was only thirty-eight years old.

Domingo, who was born in Spain but grew up in Mexico City, found a different kind of inspiration in Stanley Donen's and Gene Kelly's 1952 classic, *Singin' in the Rain.*

Gene Kelly's and Donald O'Connor's use of their bodies and the charm of both Debbie Reynolds's and Jean Hagen's acting convinced me that the magic of performing has to be a combination of many aspects and that body language is as important in winning over an audience as vocal technique. The fact that it is expected today for opera singers to move well and embody physically the characters they are portraying owes as much to musicals like *Singin' in the Rain* and *Seven Brides for Seven Brothers* as to acting lessons in conservatory.

Singin' in the Rain
Gene Kelly, 1952

"And of course in *Seven Brides* I also discovered another extraordinary voice, that of Howard Keel," says Domingo, giving a nod to another Donen classic, this one from 1954. "I've often asked myself whether the movies didn't rob the opera world of an exponent of that much sought-after voice type, the real Verdi baritone.

"In essence, I feel that the public misses a great deal of joy these days because MGM musicals are no longer fashionable."

Peter Gelb *General Manager, Metropolitan Opera*

Peter Gelb left his job as president of Sony Classical Records in 2005 to run one of the world's great opera companies. Even though he says he doesn't much like movie musicals, a film that has much influenced him in his job at the Met is one that contains a lot of music.

"*Amadeus* is a remarkably rich portrait of this genius Mozart, and the film is far better than the play," Gelb says. "Typically, the reincarnation of a work of art in another form is not as good as the original. But Milos Forman was not afraid to have extensive opera excerpts in the film, which I don't remember being effectively realized in the play. The medium of film provided a richer context, a richer palette for him to work with than the stage, and he was able to re-create the Mozart epoch. I've never seen opera filmed so dynamically, and it proves that opera can be filmed."

Using Forman's 1984 Oscar winner as his inspiration, Gelb gambled on those words that "opera can be filmed." Early in his Met tenure, Gelb began beaming live opera performances into movie theaters on a regular basis.

Regarding tuner-to-screen transfers, Gelb, who is the son of former *New York Times* managing editor Arthur Gelb, remains something of a skeptic. "None of the movie versions have stood up to the originals that I saw as a kid on Broadway and at City Center," he says. But never say never: Gelb does offer at least one caveat on that score. "*Chicago* is that rare example of a movie being equal to the musical on Broadway."

Judith Jamison *Director, Alvin Ailey American Dance Theater*

Judith Jamison refuses to pick only one movie that might have changed her life. "I've got a whole list here! First off, any musical by Busby Berkeley," she begins, reeling off the titles of such 1930s

Footlight Parade
1933

musical classics as *Footlight Parade* and *42nd Street*. "Those films had absolutely the most extraordinary dreamlike quality with all those geometric designs on the floor, such wonderful patterns that were really constructed like architecture, like building a building. But they're doing it with movement. It certainly made my cup half full instead of half empty. It always took me to another place; it was a fantasy, and how marvelous for a child to have that fantasy. [When I was] a kid, Disney World wasn't there yet. The real thing was going to movies and seeing three at a time for 75 cents."

As much as Jamison credits Berkeley, she does not forget Fred Astaire's longtime choreographer, Hermes Pan, who took on terp chores for *Top Hat,* among many other movie musicals. "I would

Chicago
Catherine Zeta-Jones, Richard Gere, and Renée
Zellweger, 2002

imitate whatever I saw Fred Astaire do, and I'd repeat it to you, his
part and his partner's," Jamison recalls. "Years later, when I was on
tour somewhere as a dancer, I met Hermes Pan. I was flabber-
gasted. I said, 'Thank You!'"

Like most kids growing up in America, Jamison didn't see
much theater, and yet she knew a dancer-choreographer idol by
way of the movies: "In *Stormy Weather,* Lena Horne is singing the
title song and Katherine Dunham and her dance company [are]
dancing around her."

Ditto the Broadway work of another great: "I first saw *Oklahoma!* and *Carousel,* with those incredible Agnes de Mille ballets, at
the movies."

As fate sometimes has it, the great American choreographer of
those Rodgers and Hammerstein classics saw the teenage Jamison

dance and brought her to New York to perform in the American Ballet Theatre, which led to an encounter with Alvin Ailey, who later cast the young dancer in his "Revelations" and created many ballets especially for her. Again, it was the movies that first introduced her to Ailey: "If you look real hard, he's dancing in *Carmen Jones,*" she says of Otto Preminger's 1954 film that put the Bizet arias in the mouths of Harry Belafonte and Dorothy Dandridge.

Jamison recently saw Josephine Baker on a DVD of Edmond T. Greville's 1935 French comedy, *Princess Tam Tam,* and vividly recalls her "singing in a bird cage with white plumes, and sparkling. Those films were fantasy and beauty. The closest they've come to that recently is *Chicago.* Somebody had the imagination to make something twinkle before our very eyes, yet it was fun. When you went outside into the real world, the world looked a little different, it changed how you felt. It's why I love theater and dance. Go see a documentary if you want to see something real."

Anna Netrebko *Soprano*

In a 2007 production of Massenet's *Manon* at the L.A. Opera, Anna Netrebko updated the eighteenth-century French courtesan to a starstruck 1950s teenager trying to impersonate the likes of Audrey Hepburn, Gina Lollabrigida, Elizabeth Taylor, and Marilyn Monroe. Despite having grown up in Communist Russia, the fiery soprano, who is often compared to Maria Callas, didn't find the acting challenge all that much of a stretch.

"When my mother was pregnant with me, she saw *Roman Holiday* and named me Anna, which is the name of the princess played by Audrey Hepburn," says Netrebko.

On the singer's career front, Hepburn's turn in the 1964 Oscar winner proved to be crucial for Netrebko. "Of course, *My Fair Lady* was the big one," she recalls. "I saw it as a young girl, and—this was before perestroika—the speaking lines were in Russian translation

My Fair Lady
Audrey Hepburn and Rex Harrison, 1964

with subtitles for the songs. But it's easy to fall in love with that music with its easy melodies and the beautiful costumes. Russians love the Hollywood musicals. They were a huge influence, but it was rare to see them. When they were on TV, the streets of the city would be empty," she says of Kasnodar, her hometown.

On her nights away from the opera house, Netrebko takes in the occasional movie tuner.

"*The Phantom of the Opera* has beautiful music, but it's a never-ending story. I'd shorten it," she says. More impressive, in her opinion, is *Chicago,* which offers not one but two femme fatale roles.

"I don't think I'm a Roxie," says the soprano. "I think I'm more the other one, Velma."

Esa-Pekka Salonen *Musical Director and Principal Conductor, L.A. Philharmonic*

"Rarely have I seen a musical film that I've liked," declares Esa-Pekka Salonen. "*Chicago* I enjoyed. It had real grit in it, and the characters felt more real despite the fact that they were singing. On stage, you don't have to be cynical when people sing about love. But in film it would be considered a banal thing to do—to simply say somebody loves somebody else. On stage, the grand feelings and enormous emotions belong to the genre somehow, which is not the case with film."

That critique aside, Salonen has nothing but praise for a very musical nonmusical film. "I saw Stanley Kubrick's *2001: A Space Odyssey* when I was ten, and it made a big impression. It played on the only wide screen in Helsinki," his Finnish hometown. More impressive than the movie's sheer size, however, was the director's achievement at matching image to music. "In my opinion, there is a moment in *2001* that is one of the greatest transitions in all of art," says the maestro.

As Salonen explains it, "When the apes learn how to use bones as tools and weapons, there is the sound of Ligeti's *Requiem,* and as the bones circle around in the air, Kubrick cuts into the image of a space station, which also rotates. The bone becomes the space station and the music cuts into 'The Blue Danube'. Many colleagues of mine, composers mainly, have mentioned *2001* as an influence, as a model for building form and transition in musical terms.

"In fact, I happened to see *2001* again a couple of months ago. I've seen it many times. It still is incredibly fresh," says Salonen. "Many sci-fi films age quickly, but the weird late-1960s look of *2001* looks futuristic again. Ten years ago, that era looked a bit awkward. But it might well be the future."

Salonen also much admires the scores that Bernard Herrmann wrote for Alfred Hitchcock's *Vertigo* and *Psycho.* "He flirts with Wagner but doesn't quite go there," he says of the composer. "Herrmann, like other movie composers, had an uncanny way of understanding image and music, especially in *Psycho* with the windshield wipers and, of course, the murder scenes.

"Music and film are both about timing," says Salonen, "and the best composers and the best filmmakers are those who are the best timers."

Michael Tilson Thomas *Music Director, San Francisco Symphony*

He conducts, composes, and plays the piano, and he is the son of Broadway stage manager Ted Thomas and the grandson of two stars of the Yiddish theater, Boris and Bessie Thomashefsky. So Michael Tilson Thomas's heart is in those movies that put the spotlight on the performer, even when those movies are as different as *Les Enfants du Paradis* and *All About Eve*.

"I first saw the Marcel Carné film when I was a romantic teenager, and I loved the idea that everyone in the movie is an artist who is in love with someone who wasn't in love with him," says the conductor-composer. The way Thomas sees it, everyone in the 1945 French classic is also an actor, whether he or she be a mime, a prostitute, a thief, or a politician. "They are various kinds of performers, and it features Jean-Louis Barrault doing his preservation of the whole world of mime as it was done with an orchestra, which is a completely different understanding from what we have of it today."

Coming from a show-biz family, Thomas also knows the milieu of Joseph L. Mankiewicz's film, in which Bette Davis essays an age-sensitive Broadway star. "With *All About Eve,* Mankiewicz succeeds in creating a screenplay that is both a delightful caricature and an absolute truthful portrait of the types that exist in our business," he notes. And if his opinion isn't good enough, Thomas goes on to quote his grandmother Bessie on *All About Eve*: "The classiest piece of material to come along in a generation!"

But in the end, Thomas himself puts it best. As he explains the allure of *All About Eve,* "What would we do without all the one-liners from that movie?"

Beyond the world of actors, Thomas's movie oeuvre embraces the obsessional as well as the absurd.

"I saw *Vertigo* when I was fourteen. I knew it was very beautiful and mysterious and really demented," he recalls. "I just didn't know how demented until I saw it again when it was restored [in

All About Eve
Bette Davis and Gary Merrill, 1950

1996]. It is such a confession from Alfred Hitchcock, which you can follow in his other movies."

Thomas gets a little obsessional himself when talking about the film in which Jimmy Stewart, as a stand-in for Hitchcock, makes over Kim Novak: "The use of the color ultramarine—that motif is used again and again in so many details, including the moment in the film when Stewart is in Barbara Bel Geddes's apartment and he is about to have his vertigo attack, and under the sink there are boxes which are outlined in ultramarine."

And, of course, for a composer like Thomas, there is Bernard Herrmann's music. "The most extraordinary thing about Herrmann in *Vertigo* is not only the notes and the harmonies but his use of a particular instrument like the contrabass clarinet that seems to come from the deepest abyss," he observes. "It's a most unusual instrument that is favored in the more extravagant scores of

Schoenberg. The sheer sound of the instrument has such a quiet menace."

If ever the contrabass clarinet sends him into a funk, "or when I think the world is hopeless," Thomas finds relief in Stan Laurel's and Oliver Hardy's *The Music Box,*" the first short film (thirty minutes) to win an Oscar, in 1932. "The Sisyphean image and the utter devotion and absurdity" of pushing that piano up a flight of stairs in the Silver Lake district of Los Angeles gets to Thomas every time. In his opinion, the two great comedians are sublime, but it's the uncredited work of character actor Billy Gilbert in the role of Prof. von Schwarzenhoffen that sends Thomas into paroxysms of laughter. "He is astonishing in the movie as the professor whom Laurel and Hardy meet halfway up the stairs," says Thomas, who acts out the following scene, complete with German accent:

Gilbert asks, "When are you numbskulls going to get out of my way?" Laurel responds, "Why don't you walk around?" And Gilbert says, "Me, walk around?!"

"That was Gilbert's specialty," says Thomas. "He was the short-fuse guy. He specialized in totally flying off."

Julie Kent *Principal Dancer, American Ballet Theater*

When producer Herbert Ross interviewed Julie Kent for his 2000 dance film, *Center Stage,* he asked what movie had made the greatest impact on her life. Kent surprised him by mentioning *Breaker Morant,* a film about the Boer War. Maybe it helped that Kent's mother had been born in New Zealand; regardless, the young dancer found herself mesmerized by the film's centerpiece: a trial in which Australian lieutenants are sentenced for executing their prisoners. Kent's imagination responded deeply to the complicated moral terrain of Bruce Beresford's 1980 film.

"I'd never seen a film about a true story where the people on trial were killed by a firing squad," she notes. "I believe that film was the beginning of a loss of innocence for me. But when a little piece of you is taken away, it actually opens another space and makes a mark on your conscience."

Another war film also left her markedly changed. "At the moment I saw *Platoon,* my brother was in the Marines," she says of Oliver Stone's Oscar-winning Vietnam-era drama, released in 1987. "In that film there is the play of right and wrong in every moment. It is not contrived drama or romantic drama. It is real drama. I was eighteen when I saw *Platoon,* and I was very much still growing up."

For Kent, who spends her days at the barre wearing a leotard and toe shoes, the macho motif just doesn't stop—at least at the movies. "Clint Eastwood's *Unforgiven* also spoke to me, that drama between what's right and wrong. I had a lot of conflicting feelings about that Western, but those are the movies I remember. They mean something to me."

For a tonic from all the aforementioned rough-and-tumble moral decisions, Kent does break form to revel in Rob Reiner's 1987 romantic fantasy, *The Princess Bride.* "For all the innocence you lost in those other films, you regain it when you are watching something like that, which is more along the lines of the stories in my work," Kent says, referring to the lead roles she essays in such classical ballets as *Sleeping Beauty, Cinderella, Giselle,* and *Swan Lake.*

This ballerina admits having seen the big dance movies, from *Red Shoes* to *West Side Story,* but in some ways they're too familiar and don't offer the needed respite from her day job. Also, "I saw them on TV years after they were made," she notes. "The big screen makes a bigger impact."

James Conlon *Music Director, L.A. Opera*

He's what they called a child prodigy. Or at least a teen prodigy. The fourteen-year-old James Conlon already knew five Mozart operas by the time he saw Albert Finney and Joyce Redman go at it with everything from peaches to clams on the half-shell in Tony Richardson's Oscar-winning *Tom Jones* in 1963. "I guess it pushed the envelope," he says of the famously sexy eating scene. "But then I hadn't pushed the envelope yet."

It's perfectly logical that a conductor of classical opera would call *Tom Jones* a most influential film, at least as Conlon explains it:

> I love Mozart more than anything. And there's something in the film's courtly manners and intrigues and these costumed people throwing themselves out of windows and hiding in closets that reverberated for me. It was alive for me. The harpsichord theme that runs through the film is delightful and a little like a classical opera, which is constructed with a dramatic situation, and then there's a moment of reflection in a duet or an aria. I found it hilarious. It is the novel put on screen, and I can't think of a single superfluous scene in it.

Conlon can almost chart his entire music career through the movies he most admires.

"I love Ingmar Bergman, and if I had to pick one it would be *The Seventh Seal,*" he says. "To go from comedy to dense, cosmic dramas—that's extreme but it reflects my musical world. I'll conduct Mozart and Haydn and then conduct Mahler and Wagner."

Regarding Bergman's 1957 masterpiece, "It hit me hard," says Conlon. "First and foremost is his penetrating look into humans and our souls and our complicated lives and the meaning of that life. I was brought up as a Catholic, and so that image of the silence and no answer coming back, no deity out there, it struck me strongly. I love the Middle Ages visually—the old tapestries, the pictures of medieval life. Maybe that's part of the appeal of *The Seventh Seal*: the grim reaper, the chess game, the dance of death at the end. Those images were powerful for me, and I was haunted by them."

Closer to Conlon's home is Francis Ford Coppola's 1972 Oscar winner, *The Godfather*. On one of his opera tours of Europe, Con-

Tom Jones
Albert Finney, 1963

lon visited the little village in southern Italy from which his great-grandparents emigrated in the late nineteenth century. "I grew up in New York City and went to high school in the Bronx; I knew that neighborhood where Michael [Al Pacino] shoots the police officer," he notes.

> I walked under that [elevated train] thousands of times as a
> kid. So *The Godfather* is my feeling of roots in New York
> City. And I'm moved by the immigrant experience. The film
> turns our feelings and perspective of a subject upside-down,
> which is the opportunity that is open to any creative artist.
> Some artists have specialized in it—Gore Vidal in particular.
> He'll take the other side of history, like Julian or Burr, and

The Godfather
James Caan, Marlon Brando, Al Pacino, and John Cazale, 1972

say, "No, this is the other side. This is what it really is." In a way, the success of *The Godfather* is to take an element in society that is criminal and yet humanize it. There's real tragedy in the father [Marlon Brando] and in the young Michael, who wants to get out and can't.

9

THE FIXERS

"I remember that movie so clearly, and thought,
'What is the meaning of life?' I realized that it is a carnival like *Ali Baba and
the Forty Thieves*. I'm sure it influenced me, later in my life, to look into
the hidden dimension of our existence."
—*Deepak Chopra*

Dr. Sanjay Gupta *Neurosurgeon*

It isn't brain surgery. Yet, watching movies can mean a lot to a second-generation Indian American growing up in small-town America (Chelsea, Michigan), where the name Gupta is about as exotic as it gets.

"I love the rah-rah movies like *Rocky* and *Remember the Titans*. They're the classic underdog stories," says the Atlanta-based neurosurgeon, who moonlights as a health correspondent for CNN. "In Philadelphia, I've run up the *Rocky* stairs," he admits.

Equally inspiring is the true story of coach Herman Boone, played by Denzel Washington in the 2000 film *Remember the Titans*. "It's about a school in the early 1970s that is racially integrated, and one of the characters [Gerry Bertier, played by Ryan Hurst] is a paraplegic who goes on to win a gold medal in the Special Olympics. It's not so much the rebelliousness of those heroes, but it's their spirit: 'Don't tell me that certain things are excluded to me.'"

Gupta's small-town midwestern life made watching Steven Spielberg's *E.T.* an especially indelible childhood experience. "I didn't get outside my town, much less planet, and the idea that we

Remember the Titans
Denzel Washington, 2000

Life Is Beautiful
Giorgio Cantarini, Roberto Benigni, and Nicoletta Braschi, 1997

are smaller than we think we are in this solar system—that's what that movie meant to me," he says. "For a young child, it gave me a sense of perspective. There is other life out there. It made that a possibility."

Growing up in the 1970s, Gupta knew too well the stereotypical professions for Indian Americans: "doctor, engineer, or owner of a 7-11. Not the movies or TV reporting," he notes. But then Gupta had a head start in the he-who-comes-first department: his mother was the first woman to be hired as an engineer by the Ford Motor Company.

Two other influential movies relate to the doctor's professional and personal life.

Gupta saw Roberto Benigni's Oscar-winning *Life Is Beautiful* when it was released in 1998 and once again more recently. "I found it even more emotionally powerful now that I have two kids of my own," he says. "What that father did for his son! The father endangers his own life in the World War II concentration camp so that his son can survive. That's the ultimate for any parent, to sacrifice themselves in that way."

On the medical front, Gupta finds Randa Haines's 1991 feature, *The Doctor,* to be more than authentic: "William Hurt plays a doctor who has been hard-charging, always the guy in charge, and then he becomes the patient and finds that he is vulnerable. I've never been in that position of being the patient for a long period of time. The movie reminds us that we are all potential patients. We can get sick and be at the mercy of people whom we don't know. It's an awful feeling."

Dr. Phil McGraw *Psychologist*

The TV shrink known as Dr. Phil calls his taste in movies "eclectic," if not downright "schizophrenic." He enjoys films with a strong psychological edge, whether they be ones he saw as a kid,

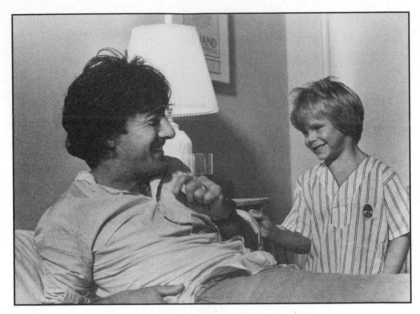

Kramer vs. Kramer
Dustin Hoffman and Justin Henry, 1979

like *12 Angry Men* and *Psycho,* or more recent fare. *"The Devil Wears Prada* is a movie about how we define ourselves," he says. "Do you sell out for someone else's definition of success?"

Dr. Phil also enjoyed Jason Reitman's 2005 satire based on Christopher Buckley's book *Thank You For Smoking.* Aaron Eckhart's portrayal of the lobbyist antihero is especially dead on, in the doctor's opinion. "It's so hard to really capture a realistic, psychologically salient character, and that was brilliant, a really good depiction of the hypocrisy of that entire industry," he says.

Which brings Dr. Phil to a top classic pick from 1971: *"Play Misty For Me* showed this psycho woman [Jessica Walter] going after Clint Eastwood, and she would call to entrap him. I've dealt with those patients who have that sort of crisis in their lives. *Play Misty For Me* was really well done. It wasn't schmaltzy or melodramatic, it was so realistic."

Regarding more typical domestic dramas, he says he'd "rather have root canal" than watch any of those movies that impress many other shrinks: *Kramer vs. Kramer, The War of the Roses,* or *Who's Afraid of Virginia Woolf?*

"Those films are well done," he begins, "but I grew up in a highly volatile home. My dad was a severe alcoholic. And I did not find movies based on that kind of conflict interesting. It's not what I go to a movie for. I could go home and watch that."

Likewise, despite having worked for Oprah Winfrey as a trial psychologist on her Texas beef trial in 1998, Dr. Phil never harbored any particular affinity for Martin Ritt's 1963 scathing indictment of a corrupt cattle rancher, played by Paul Newman. "I've seen *Hud,*" he notes. "I grew up in that part of the country. I was around that sort of thing, the oil and the cattle and the ranches and the blue jeans and the cowboy boots and the Cadillacs. It didn't have an impact. If you live it every day, it's just life. It doesn't expand your horizon."

Much more significant, to him, was Stanley Kramer's *Judgment at Nuremberg* from 1961, in which four German judges are tried for Nazi war crimes by Spencer Tracy's American judge. "I saw it when I was in the sixth grade, and at the time my experience of life extended to the nearest corner," says Dr. Phil. "You think you're the center of the universe. But with that movie and its documentary depiction of this tremendous human suffering and loss of life and the trial, it really broadened my perception of the world. I was ignorant. Everything that goes on in this world was suddenly not all happening at my school and the Little League. The movie had a really big impact on my life."

Raoul Felder *Divorce Lawyer*

His is the name that every wealthy man dreads finding on his ex-wife's speed dial. In short, Felder is America's go-in-for-the-kill king of divorce and author of *Bare Knuckle Negotiation*. This shark of split has made rich divorcees of names like Scorsese, Carson, De Palma, Gifford, and Giuliani.

"There have been so many. It's a cast of thousands," Felder says of his client roster. "And then there was what's-her-name, the Brazilian Bombshell [Bianca Jagger], who was with Mick Jagger. They all did OK."

Of split flicks, Felder says the gold standard would have to be Robert Benton's 1979 Oscar winner, *Kramer vs. Kramer*. "The film's only shortcoming was that it emphasized more what people *do* rather than what they *feel*," he says of the film's battling couple, Dustin Hoffman and Meryl Streep, both of whom took home Academy Awards. "There are so many tendrils of emotions that go through divorce cases. But *Kramer vs. Kramer* has done it better than any other film I know."

Felder also praises Danny DeVito's 1989 black comedy, *The War of the Roses*, which pits Kathleen Turner against Michael Douglas; he says it accurately depicts the "acting out" that takes place in divorce cases. "It wasn't hyperbole in terms of the anger," he says. "I've had murders take place in [divorce] cases. There were scenes in *The War of the Roses* with a pet—I had a kitten [in one divorce case] that was put in a dishwasher and a little puppy in a microwave. The puppy died. The kitten lived. I've had a case where they threatened to kill the mynah bird."

But in Felder's opinion, Turner and Douglas or Hoffman and Streep cannot compete with Elizabeth Taylor and Richard Burton in Mike Nichols's 1966 free-for-all *Who's Afraid of Virginia Woolf?* Felder calls that drama a "mutual-destruction movie. There's a scene where they bare their fangs and anger at each other—it doesn't have the label of divorce on it, it has the destruction between human relationships." Felder notes that the crackling, bruising Edward Albee dialogue, however, doesn't reflect how his clients really speak. "'Drop dead, you dirty pig.' That's the level that even high-class divorces are met with," he notes.

Who's Afraid of Virginia Woolf?
Elizabeth Taylor, 1966

As much as Felder likes these films, none of them has drastically changed his life. That distinction would arguably go to the movie that made Humphrey Bogart a major star, in 1941. From his youth growing up in Brooklyn, Felder vividly recalls *The Maltese Falcon,* which also happened to be John Huston's directorial debut. "People were able to have the zippy dialogue and look cool," he says. "It was great stuff. Everybody wanted to be like Humphrey Bogart, dangling cigarettes from their mouth. You have a generation of people with lung cancer because of that movie."

Felder repeats one favorite line from *The Maltese Falcon*; it has come to summarize his career in law. "When Sydney Greenstreet says, 'and a dollar of this is worth $10 of talk,' this is coin of the realm," he says. "I think of that often when I do negotiations."

For lawyers, Felder thinks the ultimate guilty-pleasure film of all time is Billy Wilder's 1966 comedy, *The Fortune Cookie,* in which an ambulance-chasing lawyer (Walter Matthau) convinces

The Maltese Falcon
Humphrey Bogart, Peter Lorre, Mary Astor,
and Sydney Greenstreet, 1941

his brother-in-law (Jack Lemmon) to fake an injury. "It struck a funny bone because this is so typical of a certain kind of lawyer with their phony accents," Felder observes. "I smile to myself whenever I think of that movie. I was at a party where Jack Lemmon was playing the piano at Bobby Short's house, and I told him, of all the films he ever made, this was the greatest. He played the victim there."

But it was Matthau who won the Oscar.

Dr. Drew Pinsky *Physician*

For Dr. Drew, host of the self-help *Loveline* and *Celebrity Rehab,* the prescription for a near-death experience at age fifteen was what any teenager would want: to catch a movie.

In 1973, the young Pinsky and two high school friends had spent the weekend lost in the mountains outside Los Angeles, and to celebrate their survival and return to civilization, the trio went to see William Friedkin's horror film *The Exorcist.*

"It seemed like the thing to do after being lost," he says, "but I didn't realize *The Exorcist* would take me from chronic anxiety to full-blown post-traumatic stress syndrome! I didn't sleep for about a week."

The romantic side of the doctor's brain was activated a few years later by another iconic film from the 1970s, Woody Allen's *Manhattan.* "The romance of Manhattan, the romantic flavor of longing and the very context of the city, all created very vivid feelings for me," he says, thinking back to his college days. "I liked the film because I saw it at a time when I was also feeling the emerging romantic impulses of youth that are hard to understand."

Manhattan, which opens memorably with a montage of the Gotham cityscape as set to George Gershwin's "Rhapsody in Blue," is just one of several Allen movies that Dr. Drew admires: "I love his films for their ability to beautifully capture time and place, not just because of their crazy, pathological qualities."

Deepak Chopra *Founder, The Chopra Center*

Growing up in 1950s India, Deepak Chopra saw *Ali Baba and the Forty Thieves* one afternoon with his grandfather, and later that day they went to a carnival. When they got home that night, the phone rang and it was Chopra's father, Krishna, calling from England where he was a student. The good news: Krishna Chopra had passed all his exams at the Royal College of Physicians. "My grandfather got so excited he took a rifle and shot [it] into the sky and then dropped dead. He was cremated the next day," Chopra recalls. "It is strange. I remember that movie so clearly, and thought, 'What is the meaning of life?' I realized that it is a carnival

Gandhi
Ben Kingsley, 1982

like *Ali Baba and the Forty Thieves*. I'm sure that movie influenced me, later in my life, to look into the hidden dimension of our existence."

In the following years, Chopra enjoyed *The Ten Commandments, Lawrence of Arabia,* and *Dr. Zhivago,* but the ultimate movie epic, for him, remains the 1982 Oscar winner, *Gandhi*. He knew all about Mahatma Gandhi. Even so, to see Richard Attenborough's biopic "reinforced a particular consciousness. It was great to see those stories visually represented. It was emotional. I had a kind of reawakening to the realization that courage can mean so many things, that this kind of courage actually requires more strength. We usually associate courage with war, and we give medals to those who kill the most people." *Gandhi,* of course, speaks to a different form of courage. "It's the courage of Dr. Martin Luther King Jr. and Nelson Mandela. *Gandhi* was a powerful influence for my perception of what it really means to be a hero."

Chopra's own life story as a best-selling author (*Buddha: A Story of Enlightenment*) and a leader of the transcendental movement came to the movies in summer 2008 in the form of Mike Myers's spoof, *The Love Guru,* in which the doctor-philosopher plays a cameo. That favor is returned with Chopra's new novel, *Why Is God Laughing?,* which is the story of "a comedian who tells jokes to hide his existential despair."

10

THE SHOW PEOPLE

*"I saw James Cagney in Yankee Doodle Dandy when I was five,
and his dynamic performance was thrilling, to say the least.
I'd never seen such charisma and resonance and charm."*
—*John Travolta*

Patti LuPone *Singer-Actress*

Patti LuPone had been tap dancing for four years when, at age ten, she saw Disney's *Swiss Family Robinson* in 1960. It was the movie that sealed her fate. "I marched out of that theater determined to be Tommy Kirk's leading lady," says the actress. Kirk, John Mills, Dorothy McGuire, James MacArthur, and Kevin Corcoran comprised the shipwrecked family that, because they lived in a tree in a tropical island paradise, stayed together and inspired a generation of children who'd begun to outgrow their Mouse ears and raccoonskin caps.

Although LuPone has made her career on the stage—she opened Andrew Lloyd Webber's *Evita* on Broadway in 1979 and created the role of Norma Desmond in the composer's stage version of *Sunset Boulevard* in London in 1993—movies were arguably the far greater influence on her future career. "The movies are larger than life," she opines. "They were what I watched when I was a kid, which is when you're most susceptible."

The early 1960s saw the release of two other classics that top LuPone's list of the most memorable and influential movies.

West Side Story
Natalie Wood, 1961

"To this day when I see *West Side Story* I cry my eyes out," she says. "It is the Leonard Bernstein score, the Stephen Sondheim lyrics, the Jerome Robbins choreography, the Arthur Laurents book. I don't care that Natalie Wood and Richard Beymer aren't singing with their own voices. I didn't even know the story of Shakespeare's *Romeo and Juliet* when I first saw *West Side Story*," LuPone says of the musical's source material. "I am swept off my feet with that movie and put into another world."

Directors Robert Wise and Jerome Robbins shared credit and won Oscars, but the latter helmer, who directed, choreographed, and conceived the show for Broadway in 1957, was ultimately fired from the movie project. Reportedly, he didn't stick to the strict work schedule. None of which matters to LuPone. "He knew what he was doing. Jerome Robbins was a theater director. He succeeded because he was a theater director," she says. "Too often film directors who've rarely seen stage musicals try to direct a musical, and of course it's going to be a failure. And then they blame that failure on the cast. Well, the actors don't edit the film!"

After the adventure of *Swiss Family Robinson* and the romance of *West Side Story,* LuPone found herself overwhelmed by what many consider to be the best film of the 1960s. "I didn't understand these people in the desert," she says of David Lean's 1962 epic, *Lawrence of Arabia,*

> and the film got me interested in politics. Isn't it the spoils of World War I that have created the mess for today? The problems in *Lawrence of Arabia* have come home to roost. That's what's heartbreaking about the movie, and it's all there in Peter O'Toole's face when he realizes what his government really sent him out there in the desert to do. Then there's the betrayal of all those tribes who don't care about the United Arab Republic. I was only twelve at the time I saw the film, and yet its message has never left me.

Neither has the film's stagecraft. "In *Lawrence of Arabia,* there's Omar Shariff's long, long entrance on a camel in the desert," she says. "*That* has to be the best entrance on film ever!"

Harvey Fierstein *Actor-Playwright*

One play, two Tonys. In 1983, *Torch Song Trilogy* won its creator-star, Harvey Fierstein, Broadway's top awards for best actor and play—a double-header feat never equaled in theater history.

As its show-biz title suggests, *TST* is a work that might never have been written if little Harvey hadn't sat around all day watching movies when he should have been studying math and science in grade school.

"I was a fat Jewish kid in Brooklyn who had this whole black-and-white world of movies that I loved," he recalls.

> In New York back then, they had *The Million Dollar Movie* on TV, and they showed the same movie at nine A.M., noon, three, six, and nine at night. I had to be sick from school the day they showed *Stage Door* with Katharine Hepburn and Ginger Rogers and Lucille Ball. All those women! I couldn't go to school. I loved the snappy talk, the witty banter. People didn't talk like that in Brooklyn. That sophistication, it made me crazy. It also influenced my early plays, these wise-cracking women. You could fucking die from that dialogue, it was so fast-paced!

If the 1937 Gregory La Cava–directed movie caused him to skip school, another backstage, backstabbing story, directed by Joseph L. Mankiewicz and starring Bette Davis in 1950, taught the young Fierstein everything he needed to know about the world he would come to know best. "*All About Eve* and *Stage Door* were both about show business," he says, as if to note that his other two Tonys—best actor for *Hairspray* and book writer for *La Cage aux Folles*—were for stage vehicles about performers. And both *Stage Door* and *All About Eve* starred strong women who played actresses. What else is there to say?

"I was always gay," says Fierstein. "I was not a confused child. I had baby dolls. When I put on the soundtrack to *Oklahoma!,* I did not sing, 'Oh, What a Beautiful Morning.' I sang, 'I'm Just a Girl Who Can't Say No.' I was Bette Davis, not Maurice Chevalier."

The other gay thing about young Fierstein is that he always displayed great taste and did not worship at the altar of camp when confronted with real quality: "If I had to choose between the Marx Brothers and Maria Montez in, say, *Cobra Woman,* I went for the witty dialogue of the Marx Brothers."

The gay stereotype goes only so far. For instance, it was Mr. Fierstein, and not Mrs., who mentored him in the facts of life according to 20th Century Fox. "I was my father's son," he says. "My father loved the weepy movies and was a huge fan of Barbara Stanwyck and Jane Wyman. We watched *Stella Dallas* (1937), *Sorry, Wrong Number* (1948), *Johnny Belinda* (1948), and *The Blue Veil* (1951)."

Not that there wasn't also a certain butch element to the young Fierstein's celluloid education. "I played cowboys and Indians because some of those cowboys, like Randolph Scott, were hot!" he surmises. "Also, I wanted to be an Indian when I was a kid. Jay Silverheels, who played Tonto in the *Lone Ranger* TV series, lived in Brooklyn not far from my friend Arthur. Silverheels had his garage door painted with Indian designs, which was very exotic for Flatbush."

Whatever Happened to Baby Jane?
Joan Crawford and Bette Davis, 1962

And like most red-blooded American boys, Fierstein liked the sight of it: "I had a whole fascination with bloody horror films, and we used to put on these murder mysteries in the basement." Influences for these premature thespian endeavors included *The Fly* (1958), *The Blob* (1958), *The House on Haunted Hill* (1959), and, a little later in Fierstein's development, *Whatever Happened to Baby Jane?* (1962) and *The Haunting* (1963).

As a kid, "I never hated anything about Hollywood," he says. But as an adult, "I talked my friends into seeing that remake of *The Haunting* (1999) with Liam Neeson, and now it was all special effects. I was so angry that they ruined that movie."

Fantasia *Singer-Actress*

What Broadway musicals did Fantasia absolutely love before she was approached to star in *The Color Purple* on the Great White Way?

"She had never seen a Broadway show or a musical or any theater in her entire life until we invited her to see *The Color Purple*," says the show's lead producer, Scott Sanders.

What Fantasia Barrino had done theater-wise is win *American Idol* in 2003 and tour with Jamie Foxx. Other than those on-stage assignments, she had never trained to be an actress nor had she ever really acted in *anything*. Which is not to say that the movies, among other things, hadn't prepared the singer for her 2007 Broadway debut as Alice Walker's put-upon heroine Celie.

"The movies that I grew up watching had a lot to do with singing," Fantasia says of her childhood in South Carolina.

I remember watching Diana Ross in the Billie Holliday story, *Lady Sings the Blues,* and I'd watch it over and over and over. I was curious how Billie Holliday handled things, which didn't end up good. I guess I always want to watch movies like that because I keep good people around me just

What's Love Got to Do With It
Angela Bassett, 1993

to make sure that I always keep my head on straight. Billie Holliday was so talented, so beautiful, and she had the whole world in the palm of her hands. Why did it end up that way for her? When I watch movies like *Lady Sings the Blues,* I always think, I love those women but I don't ever never want to end up like them.

Another cautionary tale that marked her is the 1993 movie *What's Love Got to Do With It,* starring Angela Bassett as the tormented Mrs. Ike Turner.

"Same thing with Miss Tina Turner," says Fantasia. "She was an amazing woman, but she had obvious issues. She had this man that she really loved but who was so disrespectful. But you know, she finally woke up! That's another movie that I used to watch all the time, over and over. You have these special women who God has given the gift of music, but behind closed doors you never know what that person's going through."

Tony Kushner *Writer*

Tony Kushner's Pulitzer Prize–winning AIDS drama, *Angels in America,* runs the gamut of Gay Legit 101, with its references to William Inge, Harvey Fierstein, and, just for good measure, Tallulah Bankhead. His screenplay for *Munich* (written with Eric Roth) puts aside any Broadway lore, however, and instead draws on Kushner's considerable film history. To write Steven Spielberg's exposé of the Black September aftermath, in which the perpetrators of the 1972 Munich Olympics massacre were systematically assassinated, Kushner looked back forty years to a tough spy story, adapted from a John le Carré novel and directed by Martin Ritt.

"*The Spy Who Came in From the Cold* is a film that I love," he says, "and is probably the only film I thought about specifically when I was working on *Munich,* because it is about the disintegration of a person in the midst of a really ambiguous, complicated, and dark situation. I was in high school when I first saw it and was really unnerved by Richard Burton's performance. What I remember about it is how it just gets grimmer and grimmer and harder and harder. I was very moved by that."

In addition to *Angels in America,* Kushner's plays *Homebody/ Kabul* and *Slavs!* have been praised for elevating agitprop to art. He believes in the Big Message, a lesson learned from another favorite film in his movie-going oeuvre.

"I really loved *The Battle of Algiers,*" he says of Gillo Pontecorvo's 1966 film about the Algerian revolution. "I've seen it several times now, and I like the way it has a clear, anticolonial political message, which is dealt with very evenhandedly. It's sometimes surprising how sympathy is divided out in the film. I also like the way that it tells very small stories and very big stories at the same time."

Anika Noni Rose *Actress*

Moviegoers know Anika Noni Rose as the Dreamgirl who is not Beyoncé or Jennifer Hudson. Broadway audiences know her as the actress who pulled off the most spectacular role reversal in recent memory, playing the adolescent Emmie in Tony Kushner's and Jeanine Tesori's *Caroline, or Change* (and winning a Tony Award in the process) and, only four short seasons later, playing the sultry Maggie in Tennessee Williams's *Cat on a Hot Tin Roof*.

Seeing the movies *The Wizard of Oz* and *The Wiz* as a kid did not make Rose want to be an actress. Nor did seeing *The Phantom of the Opera* on Broadway. "I was into science. I wanted to be a veterinarian," says the girl from Bloomfield, Connecticut. The movie *Fame,* however, did play a part in depriving New England critters of another Doctor Dolittle.

"I saw *Fame* and I wanted to go to that school!" Rose says of Alan Parker's 1980 tuner, set in Manhattan's High School for the Performing Arts. "My God, singing and dancing and flipping through the streets and on the lunch tables! What could be more fun than that?"

Despite the movie magic, Rose remained indifferent to a career on the boards—until her mother bought the *Fame* soundtrack. "I knew the songs, and when they did the stage musical *Fame* at my high school, I thought, I can do that, and I got cast as Coco, the Irene Cara role." Bye-bye, cats and dogs.

"That's when the bug bit me. I felt something I'd never felt before. It was an amazing feeling to be on stage. It was a grand eye-opener for me," she recalls.

More than its function as an audition primer, the movie *Fame* provided Rose with a huge validation. "*Seinfeld* and *Friends* are great, but they're set in New York City and they have no black friends," Rose points out. "Everybody was in *Fame*. You had Irene Cara and Debbie Allen, Latinos and Jews. That's New York! That's exciting! It was such a mishmash of everybody."

The impact of *Fame* was reinforced by *The Wiz*. Rose knew that story very well. "Every year I watched *The Wizard of Oz* on TV. It was my full-out favorite musical. My Dad would play the Lion for me and sing, and it cracked me up," she says, imitating Bert Lahr's inimitable glottal effect. "*Glglglgl!* Who would think to sing like that?" She doesn't know exactly why Dad never essayed the Scarecrow or the Tin Man. Maybe because the Lion is the funniest role in the movie, opines Rose. "He was a big gruff sissy. He just wanted to be a house cat, he didn't want to be in the forest. There are no lions in the forest, but that's a whole other conversation."

Later, Rose saw *The Wiz* starring Diana Ross as Dorothy and Michael Jackson as the Scarecrow. It didn't matter that Sidney Lumet's 1978 musical had been panned by the critics. "Michael Jackson was beautiful," she says, "and I felt that I could be part of that world, which was such a wonderful fantasy. With *The Wiz* we were allowed to have a fantasy. There's something about seeing people who look like you in the movies that feels so inclusive."

Rose says she still enjoys watching *The Wizard of Oz:* "I love that journey. *The Wiz* is a different journey with people who look like someone in my family."

John Travolta *Actor*

Although he has made only two movie musicals in his thirty-plus-year career, *Grease* in 1978 and *Hairspray* in 2007, John Travolta has been put through terp chores in some of his most memorable vehicles, including *Saturday Night Fever, Urban Cowboy,* and *Pulp Fiction,* among others. Is he surprised that dancing has emerged as part of his movie iconography?

"Not at all," Travolta says:

I saw James Cagney in *Yankee Doodle Dandy* when I was five, and his dynamic performance was thrilling, to say the

Yankee Doodle Dandy
James Cagney, 1942

least. Shortly after that my sister did *Gypsy* with Ethel Merman, and from early on I had a tremendous dose of musical theater performed at its best. But Cagney was this freak of nature with that performance. I'd never seen such charisma and resonance and charm. And it wowed me knowing that shows like *West Side Story* and *Gypsy* were possible. I especially remember being captivated by [Mazeppa], the stripper in *Gypsy,* with her number "You Gotta Have a Gimmick." So I'm not surprised that dancing is synonymous with what I do. I am an actor first, but I was always taking voice and dance lessons. I had such a passion for it, and dancing was part of my ability to entertain.

Before the movies discovered Travolta, he performed in such Broadway shows as *Over Here!* and *Grease,* and it was at a *Jesus*

Christ Superstar audition in 1971 that Robert Stigwood first spotted him. "That guy will be a star," the producer predicted, even if he didn't give him a job on the spot. That came later.

In 1977, when Stigwood and Allan Carr were putting together the *Grease* movie, Travolta asked if he could have "blue-black hair like Rock Hudson and Elvis Presley's." Nearly three decades later, Travolta not only recalls that odd fixation but also explains it: "When I was a kid, I saw those Rock Hudson and Elvis Presley movies and I loved that surrealism of blue-black hair. These guys had this almost cartoon thing about them. Black hair photographs blue, and I thought it was so authentic of the 1950s."

For Travolta's follow-up musical, *Hairspray,* the actor harbored far greater concerns when it came to the look of his character.

"I tried to convince people that I actually was a woman," he says of the Baltimore hausfrau Edna Turnblad. "I was trying to go into new territory," he says. As for movie precedents, there aren't many: Divine, in the original 1988 *Hairspray,* wouldn't fool a traveling salesman from River City, Iowa. Linda Hunt, as Billy Kwan in Peter Weir's *In the Year of Living Dangerously,* took the thesp challenge in the opposite direction. And Dustin Hoffman in *Tootsie,* as well as Jack Lemmon and Tony Curtis in the classic *Some Like It Hot,* is a man who dresses up as a woman. "No, I didn't take from those," he says. Travolta *is* a woman in *Hairspray,* and looks it.

"Because Edna is a bigger woman, it is easier to believe she is one," Travolta says. "When you get big and old, often in life the differences in women and men are not so defined."

Travolta didn't borrow from Hoffman and company because, frankly, "I had a whole library of fantastic women from the movies to choose from," he says. His personal list included "Anita Ekberg, Sophia Loren, Elizabeth Taylor, Delta Burke all gone to flesh. They're still beautiful, but they have a semblance of the shape they had when they were younger. And if they gained 200 pounds, they'd still have a semblance of their [original] shape. Jayne Mansfield and Mae West would be others. With Edna, I just felt that if I could keep a degree of sexuality that it would emphasize the vulnerability of the character."

If Travolta was influenced by any drag performer from the movies, it was Hoffman, who used a southern accent to help conceptualize his Dorothy Michaels character in *Tootsie*. "The southern accent is, by nature, more effete," says Travolta. Likewise, "What I noticed about the Baltimore accent is that the pitch goes up by nature. It is placed in the back of the nose. I felt that placement would give a more feminine tonality."

Alfred Uhry *Writer*

Alfred Uhry has earned one Pulitzer Prize, one Oscar, and two Tonys from his famed "Atlanta trilogy," *Driving Miss Daisy, The Last Night of Ballyhoo,* and *Parade*. Like his lead characters in those works, he, too, grew up Jewish in the South, and his assimilation of the Gentile culture around him ("we had Easter eggs and Christmas trees") was due, in no small part, to the steady diet of movies he consumed as a kid.

"Those guys who were in those homogenized Andy Hardy movies—those people were pretty much what I wanted to be," he recalls. "The only Jews I saw in the movies were these Al Jolson types who lived in dark places. Every Jew I knew growing up in Atlanta, Georgia, was playing golf at some country club, so I knew in my heart that I would grow up to be like Van Johnson, who got to swim around with Esther Williams. That's what I wanted to be."

In a way, the movies also introduced Uhry to his future career. "What impressed me as a kid were those biographic movies about Broadway composers," he notes. "I thought life would be like that of Cole Porter in *Night and Day* and Richard Rodgers and Lorenz Hart in *Words and Music*. Those MGM composer biographies seemed like the most wonderful world to me. I fell in love with the idea of Broadway from the movies. In those days, Broadway was a

Gentleman's Agreement
Gregory Peck, 1947

buzzword for sophistication. It was the world I wanted to be in, like the characters in Woody Allen's *The Purple Rose of Cairo* who retreat into the world of the movies."

It was also from the movies that he learned his first lesson on how to write the book for a stage musical: "I was about eight years old when I saw *Meet Me in St. Louis.* There's the scene where Judy Garland stands by those curtains and sings that song ['The Boy Next Door'] that really isn't a song. She is singing her thoughts. I always found that interesting, and it was a real influence on my writing."

For all of their fantastical escapism, the movies did bring home the prejudice around him. Uhry can't remember if he saw the anti-Semitism classic *Gentleman's Agreement* when he was a kid in 1947. "But when I saw it as a grown man, I saw John Garfield, and there's the scene where a squad mate is wounded and begging for a medic, and the medic says, 'Somebody take care of that sheenie!' That rang a bell. I'll never forget how strong that was."

David Rockwell *Architect-Designer*

David Rockwell has designed everything from the Broadway productions of *Legally Blonde* and *Hairspray* to Las Vegas's Phantom of the Opera theater, as well as Hollywood's Kodak Theater, home of the Academy Awards.

It has been said of Rockwell that when he designs restaurants (Nobu, Bar Americain) they look like theaters, and when he designs sets, people want to eat them.

But food or theater, it all started at the movies for this architect-designer.

"*The Fountainhead* was hugely influential in my interest in design," Rockwell says of King Vidor's 1949 adaptation of Ayn Rand's camp novel. "As corny as it is," he adds.

Seeing *The Fountainhead,* coupled with an early visit to New York City in 1964 to visit the World Fair, "I knew immediately it was a place I wanted to live." It helped that Rockwell idolized Frank Lloyd Wright and that *The Fountainhead* championed modern architecture.

But it was the film's oversized look of the city that hooked Rockwell, "particularly those scenes looking out windows at Manhattan. There are some amazing power offices," he notes. "And there's one scene where Gary Cooper peels some ornamentation off a model of a minimal skyscraper. That made an impression."

Rockwell wasn't alone in his love of Rand's loner hero, Howard Roark. "Every fourth architecture student at the university had a dog named Roark," he recalls.

Manhattan lived in other films as well, and it was the extravagant musicals of Busby Berkeley that inspired Rockwell. "I liked the stylized use of Broadway in *42nd Street,*" he says. "The camera movement is of as great an interest to me as the sets. What interests me about space is people moving through it cinematically. You never perceive a space fully but rather as you move through it." Take Radio City Music Hall. "That small entry and then that huge vertical space with the staircase is as choreographed as any part of *42nd Street.*"

The futuristic past also surfaces in another adolescent pleasure for Rockwell: the design work of Ken Adam, production designer on the early James Bond films *Dr. No* and *Goldfinger.* "He combined glamour and style and a heightened reality," says Rockwell. "He built these amazing places that combined exotic parts of the world and fantasy worlds. I was struck by his interest in detail. Each piece has a backstory."

Anne Hathaway *Actress*

An "Anne Hathaway movie" has come to mean lots of fashion. *The Devil Wears Prada* required that stylist Patricia Field work overtime. *Brokeback Mountain* saw the actress change wigs for nearly every one of her scenes. The fashion fixation started early for Hathaway. Take the seminal Julia Roberts headliner *Pretty Woman,* which, along with *All That Jazz,* tops her list of influential movies.

"As a child, I understood the fairy tale aspect of *Pretty Woman* more than I understood anything about the sexual side of the film," Hathaway recalls. She took another look at the 1990 call-girl romance before working with director Garry Marshall on *The Princess Diaries.* "I rewatched the film when I was seventeen and I [realized], 'Oh my God, she's giving him a blow job in that scene.' I never picked up on that!"

Pretty Woman's appeal is universal, regardless of age or mores, Hathaway believes: "The story is something a lot of people respond to: life can get better."

Released in 1979, Bob Fosse's bitter-pill Valentine to show business, in contrast, speaks directly to Hathaway's alter ego.

"That's the world, the theater, I've always dreamed about being in, actually," she says of *All That Jazz.* "Technically, I haven't realized my childhood dreams. I don't mean to sound ungrateful

All That Jazz
Roy Scheider, 1979

for my success [in film], but I always just kind of wanted to be a hoofer on Broadway. I wanted to be up there singing and dancing, and it's always what I thought I'd be doing."

Any chance she ever will?

"The good thing about that dream not being realized," she says, "is that I would have been embarrassed. I dance passionately, but I don't think I'm a very good dancer."

11

THE WALL STREETERS

"It's all about how to monopolize a scarce resource, water,
to create an artificial crisis that you can turn to profit. *Chinatown*
really prefigures the California electric crisis of 2000–2001."
—*Paul Krugman*

James Cramer *Financial Analyst*

Tales of failed businessmen all seem straight out of a typical melo-
drama: young idealist storms into Wall Street with the best intentions, only to be chewed up and spit out by the predacious corruption
of the business world. So perhaps James Cramer's success—first as a
Wall Street kingpin, currently as an author and TV host of *Mad
Money*—can be traced to his rather unidealistic business model,
Francis Ford Coppola's 1974 Oscar winner, *The Godfather: Part II*.

"I saw that early in college," Cramer says, "and it really got me
thinking. Is business really just about power and corruption? Is the
mafia actually a model for American business in general? And that
turned out to be the case.

"I was already way too cynical," he continues, "and that movie
just made me so much more so."

Armed with dark attitude, Cramer made a fortune as a
Goldman-Sachs trader and later a hedge-fund manager in the
1980s. He also befriended future incarcerate Ivan Boesky, who inspired the Gordon Gekko character in Oliver Stone's 1987 indictment of American capitalism, *Wall Street*.

The Godfather: Part II
Lee Strasberg and Al Pacino, 1974

Cramer calls the film "totally accurate in its depiction of the raiders. And of the hedge-fund world, too, which creates no value whatsoever. This kind of vicious capitalism must be stopped. How many people does it put to work? To put it in Marxist terms, it's a friction in the system. That's why *Wall Street* was such an honest movie."

He eventually quit the hedge-fund business due to, as he describes it, "this overall sense that I truly belonged in hell." Cramer's work since in books and TV has emphasized a subversive view of investment, one nonetheless anathema to the pipe-dream populism of films like John Ford's *The Grapes of Wrath* and Frank Capra's *It's a Wonderful Life*.

"It would be absolutely fabulous if *The Grapes of Wrath* were true," he says. "You know what else would be great? If the Bailey

It's a Wonderful Life
Donna Reed and James Stewart, 1946

Building & Loan were to survive in *It's a Wonderful Life*. It would be great if Mr. Martini got his loan and Potter lost it all in the Depression," Cramer adds, quickly refashioning the Christmas classic. "But in real life we'd all be going to the Potter Library and thinking of him as a great benefactor. Potter probably would have bought off the bank examiner just to shut down the Building & Loan."

His veridicality notwithstanding, when asked if he has any guilty pleasures, Cramer cites a Steven Seagal cop potboiler from 1990: "*Hard to Kill*. Mason Storm is perhaps my favorite character ever. 'We will win because we have a superior attitude and a superior state of mind.' That's the greatest line. I've used it ten times on my show."

Donald Trump *Entrepreneur*

When Macaulay Culkin asked him directions to the main lobby, the Donald responded, "Down the hall and to the left."

That immortal line was Donald Trump's first in a movie, *Home Alone 2: Lost in New York,* and since 1992 he has essayed himself with equally stunning authenticity in *The Associate, Celebrity, Citizen Black, Eddie, Little Rascals, Marmalade, The Pickle, Two Week's Notice, Zoolander,* and more.

Billionaire (despite the claims of Rosie O'Donnell), author, and former reality-TV host, Trump shows much better taste in picking a most influential movie.

"*Citizen Kane* is sophisticated and innovative in every aspect," he says, citing the 1941 classic that many critics consider to be the best movie of all time, even though it won only one Oscar, for screenplay, by Orson Welles and Herman Mankiewicz. "Its perspective on power is compelling, as are the characters and the story line—yet, it remains enigmatic," Trump adds. "It is storytelling at its best."

Paul E. Steiger *Editor at Large, the* Wall Street Journal

"Hollywood tends to draw its villains from business, and they tend to be cartoonish, which is OK. You get your villains where you find them."

That's the expert opinion of the *Wall Street Journal*'s longtime managing editor, Paul E. Steiger, who segued to a less hands-on post in 2007. "Writers and creative people tend to have sympathy for the underdog, and business people are such obvious overdogs," he explains. "You see it even with people in Hollywood who make $20 million a picture."

Although he reserves kudos for Oliver Stone's *Wall Street* ("it did catch the excesses of the greed-is-good era"), the editor prefers

Working Girl
Melanie Griffith and Harrison Ford, 1988

it when Hollywood attacks his business-world turf with a sense of humor. "In the movies, business leaders are two-dimensional in dramas and more three-dimensional in comedies," he opines. "I don't know why that is." Steiger has examples to prove his point, picking three business comedies he especially admires.

"Sigourney Weaver was fabulous in *Working Girl*," says Steiger, thinking back to Mike Nichols's 1988 comedy about the brokers of mergers and acquisitions. "My memory of the movie is that Weaver's character probably had to struggle to get where she was; she didn't inherit the company. And here comes this blonde [Melanie Griffith] on the Staten Island ferry who is a risk not only to her position in the company but her position with her fiancé [Harrison Ford]. And so while she was vicious and hilariously conniving, it was a character that had some shading to it. Sigourney

Weaver plays tall; her face conveys intelligence. She was a worthy adversary for Melanie Griffith."

Steiger also enjoyed Aaron Eckhart in his 2006 role as a tobacco lobbyist: "In *Thank You For Smoking,* they are definitely playing for laughs, but somehow the movie lets its negative characters have some redeeming social value."

And then there is *The Devil Wears Prada:* "Meryl Streep took an over-the-top caricature of Anna Wintour from the novel and gave her a three-dimensional element. By the end of the movie, you understand the challenges of leadership in a highly competitive and sometimes backstabbing world."

Steiger can't pick any one movie that changed his life, which is not to say he minimizes the medium's power. "When I was a kid growing up in Stamford, Connecticut, which was rural then, we used to play cowboys and sing the theme music from our favorite Westerns," he recalls. "The movies so governed the way you thought about the world."

John Wayne ruled, in Steiger's opinion, but it was a Western that he saw in college in 1961 that helped to form his development as a writer and editor.

"Marlon Brando's *One-Eyed Jacks* is flawed, but it is beautifully shot and the supporting characters are some of the best actors, Katy Jurado and Pina Pellicer, two Mexican actors who took all the clichés and played against them, both embraced them and blew them up," says Steiger. "The film influenced my thinking: you don't have to be afraid of clichés if you know what you're doing, that in any storytelling you need both character and dramatic arc, and that's how the subsidiary characters played into that movie so well."

In a way, the movies also helped to develop Steiger's own sense of sexual politics. "I was at an age when I was in love with Elizabeth Taylor, and Marilyn Monroe was such a dominant figure. I didn't see what all the James Dean fuss was about. And then there were some movies that Paul Newman and Joanne Woodward

One-Eyed Jacks
Marlon Brando, 1961

starred in together in the late 1950s, early 1960s," he says, referring to *The Long, Hot Summer* and *From the Terrace*. "The chemistry between them was unbelievable, and that played into the notion that women don't have to be subservient."

Paul Krugman *Economist*

The *New York Times* financial columnist calls the celluloid triptych his "economics films." And they could hardly be more different on the surface of it: *The Man Who Shot Liberty Valance*, *Chinatown*, and *Wall Street*.

As the 2008 Nobel Prize winner sees it, John Ford's 1962 Western, which pits farmer James Stewart against cowboy John Wayne,

Wall Street
Michael Douglas, 1987

is "all about bringing property rights to the West. It's nostalgic: Wayne is the last cowboy, but the future belongs to Stewart and the forces of social organization by way of a dam."

Krugman, a neo-Keynesian who teaches at Princeton, can't understand why so few critics miss the point that Roman Polanski's 1974 noir is first and foremost a business film. "It's all about how to monopolize a scarce resource, water, to create an artificial crisis that you can turn to profit. The plot doesn't hinge on mysterious treasure; it's who's going to have control of the Southern California water supply. *Chinatown* really prefigures the California electric crisis of 2000–2001," he points out.

Oliver Stone's finance epic is "a little crude in terms of drama," says Krugman, "but the business side is dead-on." Michael Douglas's Gordon Gekko is obviously modeled on Ivan Boesky. "But

Doctor Zhivago
Julie Christie and Omar Shariff, 1965

word for word the Gekko speeches sound like what people were writing in the *Harvard Business Review* regarding stock-option pay and the practices that led to these huge executive paychecks." Krugman especially relishes the speech that Douglas gives to his protégé, played by Charlie Sheen, in which he belittles Wall Streeters who are satisfied with "flying first-class and making $400,000 a year." Says Krugman, "Most people just don't understand how rich the super-rich are today."

Krugman is a proud leftist, and to prove it he recently published a book, *The Conscience of a Liberal,* which echoes Barry Goldwater's famous 1963 tome, *The Conscience of a Conservative.* Politics and social concern, however, take you only so far at the movies, Krugman believes. As a kid, he reveled in David Lean's *Dr. Zhivago,* and he has seen the 1965 Russian epic multiple times—not for its message about the evils of Communism but its grand visual impact. "Some images have stayed with me forever, like the Cossacks charging the demonstrators and the armed trains. Kids like trains," he says.

Pauline Kael criticized the film's final image of a rainbow over a hydroelectric dam in the USSR, calling it oddly pro-Communist. Krugman is into sociopolitical arguments wherever he can find them, but he calls that assessment of *Dr. Zhivago* as downright "silly. I suppose if they rereleased *Lawrence of Arabia,* someone could say it is pro-Arab," he adds.

12

THE ATHLETES

"Being a quarterback is being a leader. Any time I don't feel
well or am stuck at home, I'm watching *Patton*."
—*Boomer Esiason*

Jerry Rice *Receiver*

As the all-time leading receiver in the National Football League,
Jerry Rice is looked upon by both Pop Warner tykes and current
NFL players as someone who fulfilled his dreams of being the best.
As he made his way up the pigskin ladder, Rice took his inspiration
from Daniel Ruettiger.

Who is Ruettiger? Most know him by his nickname, Rudy—
or *Rudy,* a 1993 release. *Hoosiers* director David Anspaugh left the
court for the field on this one, about a small-bodied but big-hearted
Notre Dame student, played by Sean Astin, who in his final game
in uniform, without previously ever getting on the field, got a
chance to go out and play defense against Georgia Tech. "You're
always going to have someone on your team not as talented as the
others, but they give 100 percent on the field each day in practice,"
Rice observes. "I've seen so many players like that. They enjoy just
being there and being part of the game."

While *Rudy* inspired Rice, his San Francisco 49ers coach Bill
Walsh screened other films to help get his team motivated. Nothing

Gladiator
Russell Crowe, 2000

worked better than Ridley Scott's 2000 Oscar winner, *Gladiator,* which was screened for the players on their march toward another Super Bowl. "The part of the film when they're in the arena, and they all have to band together, is what I take from that film," says Rice, recalling the scene where Russell Crowe leads his fellow gladiators to defeat a charge of chariot-riding archers. "If they do that, they all have a chance."

Yeah, early variations of teamwork. Roman-style.

Luc Robitaille *Left Winger*

The French-Canadian hockey great grew up in Montreal, knowing not a lick of English. But Paramount's 1978 musical phenome-

Grease
Olivia Newton-John and John Travolta, 1978

non, *Grease,* with John Travolta's black leather jacket and Olivia Newton-John's Spandex pants, spoke to Luc Robitaille just as it did to millions of others: As of 2008, *Grease* remains the top-grossing tuner of all time.

"I just thought Travolta was the coolest dude," says Robitaille, who retired in 2006 from the L.A. Kings after nineteen years in the NHL as the highest-scoring left-winger in league history. "*Grease* was showing in Quebec at this one-dollar theater that had it in English, and I went to see it six weeks in a row. I would shovel driveways to get money for the movie and popcorn."

A year earlier Robitaille and his buddies repeatedly ventured to the big screen to catch *Slap Shot,* in which Paul Newman (who called the George Roy Hill–directed movie his personal favorite) portrays an aging hockey player on a losing minor-league team.

And even though the film was released in 1977, it's still considered the definitive hockey picture, thanks to the appearance of the three Hanson brothers and the soundtrack's ultra-foul (for the late 1970s) language.

"That movie was one of the few that they translated into French," Robitaille says. "In Quebec, when you translate the English swear words, we would add about thirty more of them, so we got a kick out of it."

Regarding more recent films to unspool at the multiplex, Robitaille is an unabashed fan of one comedy: "As a family, we all loved *Little Miss Sunshine*."

And he isn't afraid to see a film—present-day or classic—that will make him shed a few tears. "My wife always laughs at me, because I'll see the chick flicks, and I enjoy them as much as anyone," he says. "I love to get some sort of emotion coming off the screen."

Boomer Esiason *Quarterback*

With a father who fought in World War II, it only made sense that Boomer Esiason would find comfort watching combat pictures with his Dad.

Esiason, one of the most successful quarterbacks in NFL history—he played the majority of his career with the Cincinnati Bengals and New York Jets—calls *Patton* his favorite film of all time. He's seen the 1970 picture, which won Oscars both for best picture and George C. Scott's lead performance, about sixty times, he estimates.

"Being a quarterback is being a leader," Esiason says, describing the similarities of Scott's role as a U.S. general and his job as an in-charge athlete on the football field. "Any time I don't feel well or am stuck at home, I'm watching *Patton*."

It's not just *Patton* that resonates with Esiason. He's a huge fan of the entire military genre and grew up being entranced with

Patton
George C. Scott, 1970

films such as *The Bridge on the River Kwai, Kelly's Heroes,* and *The Guns of Navarone.* During the past twenty years, *Apocalypse Now, Platoon, We Were Soldiers,* and *Saving Private Ryan* have all deeply affected him as well.

"I got a chance to see *Private Ryan* with my Dad before he passed away, and my son was with us too," says Esiason. "The fact that three generations could share that meant a lot. . . . My dad was very silent when we watched, and very moved. It brought back a lot of memories for him. He was in the Battle of the Bulge. Like most veterans, he never spoke much about it."

Esiason goes to the movies for pure escapism but prefers to see films that have higher aspirations. On that score, he especially enjoys Steven Spielberg's 1993 Oscar winner, *Schindler's List.*

"I like movies that teach you something about history," he says. "Whether it was the scene with the little girl in the red coat in *Schindler's List*, the commandant [Ralph Fiennes] being vicious and vile, or those who helped keep people alive, these are scenes that last with you for a lifetime."

Shannon Sharpe *Tight End*

Growing up poor in Georgia, Shannon Sharpe could never afford to go to the movies. Now, it seems, the all-time leading yardage leader for tight ends in NFL history can't afford not to.

Sharpe considers himself a movie junkie, once going to see six films in a single day—a feat even Roger Ebert wouldn't take upon himself. Retired from football in 2003, Sharpe now works for CBS Sports as a commentator and has plenty of time to see everything.

"I don't remember going to any movies as a kid, but now it's a part of my life," says Sharpe, who clocks in about seventy-five pictures a year.

The athlete has a difficult time pinpointing a life-altering film but will catch anything starring Denzel Washington, including *The Great Debaters,* which is the second film the Oscar-winning actor has directed. "It was just a great feel-good story," Sharpe explains. "You knew how it was going to end, but Denzel and Forest Whitaker were unbelievable."

The football player wouldn't rate *Debaters* at the top of his list of Washington's best films; those spots he holds for *Malcolm X,* closely followed by *The Hurricane.*

Unlike many athletes, Sharpe doesn't automatically gravitate toward sports films. Though he understands the desire for viewers to grasp what being a pro player is all about, Sharpe says his unique experience on the gridiron could never be replicated in film and he would rather see a different genre as a form of escapism. "The thing is, I played the game. I didn't need to see *Rudy, Invincible,* or *The Replacements,*" he says. "I've watched *Hoosiers* but I'm not a sports guy."

Now, as well as when he was playing, Sharpe doesn't feel the need to bring a companion along while venturing to the multiplex. Once he has his mind set on which movie to see, he prefers not to take someone as they may talk him out of seeing a certain movie.

"I like to go by myself," he reiterates. "This way, I'm assured of seeing what I want to see."

Rick Fox *Forward*

Rick Fox didn't just watch the iconic 1986 basketball film *Hoosiers,* he lived it.

The former NBA player, who won three world championships with the L.A. Lakers over a fourteen-year pro career, grew up in the Bahamas, which isn't exactly a hoops hotbed. Then he moved to Indiana during his high school years and found himself not only in *Hoosiers* country but playing with one of his teammates as a co-star in the film. The David Anspaugh–directed picture took on an even higher meaning.

"*Hoosiers* has stayed in my life on many levels," Fox explains. "I was this bright-eyed kid who had just gotten to town, and then they had the movie premiere there."

The Gene Hackman film is widely regarded as the definitive basketball movie in depicting small-town sports as well as the heroism of the underdog against bigger, and sometimes more talented, opponents.

"I remember being a part of that. It was very special," Fox recalls. "You had this opportunity to represent your town. It was pure in that you were all really rooting for each other. Once you step out of the high school arena, you lose that sense of community."

Rocky
Sylvester Stallone, 1975

Ty Murray *Rodeo Cowboy*

In his decade-long tenure as king of rodeo cowboys, Ty Murray suffered torn ligaments in both knees, major injuries and fractures in both shoulders, and a broken jaw administered by an irate bull. So it's fitting that he should draw inspiration from another oft-battered survivor athlete, Rocky Balboa.

"*Rocky* is still to this date my favorite movie," Murray says. But he's a little uneasy with that choice, forgetting, perhaps, that the Sylvester Stallone boxer movie won the top Oscar and another for its director, John Avildsen. "I guess people might look at it now and make fun of it, but at the time I saw *Rocky,* I was probably eight or nine years old," this cowboy offers with apologies. "And being a guy who wanted to be a great athlete, that movie made a huge impact on me and my career. It made me a believer from an early age that if you want something bad enough and work hard enough at it, you're going to get out of stuff what you put into it."

Somehow, the world-weary, underdog aspect of the film spoke to Murray, who never played the loser à la Rocky Balboa. In fact, this rodeo cowboy won his first competition at age five. At twenty, he became the youngest man to win the PRCA's All-Around Rodeo Cowboy title, which he went on to attain another six times, making him the winningest professional cowboy in the history of the sport.

"I don't know if it would've affected me as much at age thirty," Murray admits. "But as a young kid, *Rocky* had a bigger impact on me than any [films] have since."

Murray retired from professional competition in 2002; time will tell if he follows his hero's lead and throws his Stetson back into the ring. He claims to be a big fan of Quentin Tarantino's *Pulp Fiction* and the canon of Denzel Washington (whom Murray compares to a "modern-day John Wayne"), but the cowboy has been disappointed by Hollywood's attempts to portray the world of rodeo. And that includes the 1994 Lane Forest biopic, *8 Seconds,* for which he script-consulted. "It's the closest a rodeo movie has come to being true to life," Murray opines, "but it's still pretty far off."

Bob Baffert *Horse Racing Trainer*

As one of the giant trainers of horse racing, Bob Baffert has won the Kentucky Derby three times, and his horses have earned more than $112 million. And who does Baffert cite as an inspiration in his phenomenal career in racing? A jockey? Fellow trainer? Nope. Charlton Heston.

Growing up in Arizona, Baffert vividly recalls seeing *Ben-Hur* at age six and can still see the iconic chariot races play in his head over and over. But it was also Heston's humane treatment of the

Ben-Hur
Charlton Heston, 1959

horses that made a subliminal impression. "I remember how he got those horses and then how he took care of them," Baffert says. "I remember it so well, seeing it with my parents."

Horses also play a big role in Baffert's all-time favorite picture, the 1990 Oscar-winning *Dances With Wolves,* in which Kevin Costner travels the Great Plains aboard an equine. And he really relates to *Phar Lap,* the 1984 film about an Australian racehorse, its real-life trainer Harry Telford, played by Martin Vaughan, "who thought he was genius. You can get lucky one time," Baffert says, laughing.

Then there's *Seabiscuit,* which inspired him in an entirely different way. The 2003 picture was partly filmed at Santa Anita, and Baffert got to know director Gary Ross, as well as become friends with jockey Gary Stevens, who played George Woolf in this true story of how athletes and animals join together to overcome all odds.

Baffert is a sucker for almost any film starring an animal, but like a lot of jocks he also has a soft side for male-dominated comedies, such as the 1975 goofball hit *Animal House,* the 1980 golf favorite *Caddyshack,* and, from 2005, *Wedding Crashers,* which, like the other two films, proves that men are animals.

Although he won't be the first to run out and catch a musical—either onscreen or onstage—*The Sound of Music* holds fond memories for Baffert. "It's the only musical I've ever liked, the only one I could watch," he says. "As a kid, I had a crush on Julie Andrews. I think everyone did."

Gov. Bill Richardson *Governor, New Mexico*

Bill Richardson came to politics relatively late in life. The New Mexico state governor and former ambassador to the United Nations first pursued a career in baseball, so it's no wonder that many of the movies that have affected him feature the sport: for example, *The Natural* (1984) with Robert Redford, and *Field of Dreams* (1989) with Kevin Costner.

"I was a baseball player," he says. But then he got into politics—and the movies had nothing to do with it. "I was inspired by two speeches. One was John F. Kennedy's inaugural speech, and the other was Hubert Humphrey, just a speech this newcomer gave about public service, about giving, and I was hooked. I was twenty-two. Most people develop their interests earlier."

The former pitcher put aside his ambitions of going pro and instead decided to pursue a political science degree at Tufts University, where he saw his all-time favorite movie, *Butch Cassidy and the Sundance Kid,* starring Paul Newman and Redford (again) as the titular outlaws, in 1969. "I've seen it a total of twenty-eight times," he says. "I love to watch films many times over because I don't want to be surprised. I like knowing the outcomes.

"Another one I really like—and it's very tied to my early days—is *Love Story* with Ali MacGraw, who, by the way, has become a very good friend," he adds. "She lives in Santa Fe."

When it comes to films about his current home turf—politics—Richardson cites Michael Ritchie's 1972 examination of the process, *The Candidate,* with Redford (yet again) playing a politician who sells out to win. "It's a wonderful depiction of the typical vacuousness of a political campaign, as well as the compromises you have to make to get elected, but it is also a funny look at our political process. While flawed, it is a good one, because it involves appealing to common people," he says.

JFK may be Richardson's ultimate hero, but the governor is clearly "a big Redford fan," since three of his favorite films star the actor.

"I'm trying to lure Redford to come establish a Sundance 2 in New Mexico," Richardson reveals, "and we've even purchased an old historic ranch in northern New Mexico for him to bring his seminars."

The movies, obviously, had something to do with that.

13

THE OPINIONMAKERS

"I saw myself as the little brother going, 'Can I tag along and
bring down the government too?' That was the feeling
I had when I left the theater after seeing *M*A*S*H*."
—*Bill Maher*

Frank Rich *Columnist, the* New York Times

The political left has found its most articulate voice in Frank Rich,
his weekly column in the *Sunday New York Times* a must-read for
political junkies of any stripe. Back in the 1980s, Rich was equally
renowned for his make-or-break theater reviews in the newspaper
of record. Rich, in fact, has been such a towering figure at the
Times for so long that his earlier career in the 1970s as a film reviewer for *New Times,* the *New York Post,* and then *Time* has been
almost forgotten.

At the *Harvard Crimson,* Rich began to write about his first
love, the theater, when an upperclassman cautioned him, "The theater is dying, you'd better learn how to be a film critic." That upperclassman, Tim Hunter, went on to direct episodes of *Law &
Order* and *Mad Men,* and Rich, who initially took Hunter's advice,
has critiqued everyone from Coppola and Sondheim to Bush and
Obama in the course of his career.

In his 2001 memoir, *Ghost Light,* Rich writes about growing
up in a broken home in Washington, D.C., and how the theater
provided both an escape from his troubled adolescence and a

pathway to his adult vocation. It was the movies, however, that led him to dream about the theater's ghost light. "I saw *Singin' in the Rain* when I was three. I must have seen it when it was re-released," he says of the 1952 movie classic. "With its joyous view of musical comedy and its broad satire, it paved the way for how exciting I would find musical comedy in legitimate theater when I was older."

Later, he saw a triptych of films that taught him about politics in a way that the theater never would. "Growing up in Washington, D.C., and being given this official version of Washington, D.C., I learned that there was something more subversive than the official version," Rich says of the films *North by Northwest, The Manchurian Candidate,* and *Dr. Strangelove.* "I found *North by Northwest* so mesmerizing that I demanded that my family take me back to see it the very next day, and they did. It was 1958; I was nine. I saw it in VistaVision at the old Loew's Palace, which no longer exists. I didn't understand the Cold War yet, but I was gripped by the story, its sweep, and the view that the surface of reality is not to be trusted. I still love the movie; and Alfred Hitchcock, if not my favorite director, is in the top two or three."

In the early 1960s, Rich saw John Frankenheimer's *The Manchurian Candidate* and Stanley Kubrick's *Dr. Strangelove.* "Again, they offered an alternate view of official Washington," he says. "I was in my adolescence now, and I understood them. I just love the issue of McCarthyism in *The Manchurian Candidate,* and the satire of the military establishment in *Dr. Strangelove* was quite something for a kid growing up in the nation's capital."

Rich's sociopolitical sensibilities were further honed by *The Twilight Zone,* Mort Sahl, *Mad* magazine, and Lenny Bruce, and his developing aesthetic led him to the films of François Truffaut and Michelangelo Antonioni. "But not Ingmar Bergman. I never responded to Bergman. When I was in high school, in rapid succession, I saw *Jules and Jim* and *Blowup,* which introduced me to modern European filmmaking and to what I came to know as the

Bonnie and Clyde
Faye Dunaway and Warren Beatty, 1967

new wave. I saw movies differently." He didn't feel that contemporary American movies could ever measure up—until Arthur Penn directed *Bonnie and Clyde*: "It captured the rebellion that was brewing in American life, and it captured some of the European new wave. It was so unlike any American studio movie I'd ever seen. Finally, American movies could have these subversive qualities of the new cinema in Europe."

Stanley Kubrick's *2001: A Space Odyssey* followed shortly after *Bonnie and Clyde,* in 1969, and it, too, impressed: "I was a freshman at Harvard, and seeing *2001* sober—that kind of major Hollywood movie with visual storytelling at such a high level with no dialogue for acres of that movie—it was a breakthrough, and it changed my taste."

Peggy Noonan *Columnist, the* Wall Street Journal

In his seminal tome on the original Hollywood moguls, *An Empire of Their Own,* Neal Gabler chronicles "How the Jews Invented Hollywood." Not many of those films from the 1920s through the 1940s dealt with the Jewish experience in America. Louis B. Mayer, Harry Cohn, Jack Warner, and Adolph Zukor left it to the Gentile among them, Darryl F. Zanuck, to make the breakthrough *Gentleman's Agreement,* in 1947, about anti-Semitism. But Mayer and company did make a lot of movies about another immigrant group, and Peggy Noonan would like to take this opportunity to salute them.

"I always wanted to give thanks to the great movie studio titans of the 1920s–1950s, the men who invented Hollywood, who could not resist making the Irish of America look like the most wonderful people in the world," says the woman who wrote a few speeches delivered by her fellow Irish American Ronald Reagan. "The Irish they showed in the movies were brave, beautiful, humorous, stirring. That message was not lost on a young Irish American in Massapequa, Long Island."

As a kid, Margaret Ellen Noonan saw most of those films— some directed by John Ford, some starring James Cagney—on New York City's Channel 9 program *The Million Dollar Movie.* And she'd like to thank those programmers, too. "God bless them for giving so much great art to the children of New York through the 1950s and 1960s."

Her favorite Irish-American motion picture: *Yankee Doodle Dandy,* starring Cagney and directed by Hungarian émigré Mano Kertesz Kaminer, a.k.a. Michael Curtiz. Noonan fondly relives the moment "when Cagney's George M. Cohan receives a presidential medal from FDR and gives his speech: 'My mother thanks you, my father thanks you, my sister thanks you. . . .'"

"Oh my goodness!" exclaims Noonan.

It's doubtful that her old boss The Gipper would find much to criticize in Noonan's Long Island girlhood, with its positively upbeat diet of Westerns and World War II movies. They made her the proud political conservative who, after the Reagan years, went on to write *A Heart Is a Cross and a Flag* and *Life, Liberty, and the Pursuit of Happiness.* Recalling *Stagecoach, She Wore a Yellow Ribbon, Rio Grande,* and *The Searchers,* Noonan lauds the films of the man who won more Academy Awards (four) than any other director and, born John Martin Feeney, just happened to be Irish American:

"John Ford had clearly internalized, and immortalized in his work, a particular style of masculinity: strong, keenly observant, resourceful, seeking meaning in actions, not words. This would include just about all the roles John Wayne played for him, and Henry Fonda's work in *The Grapes of Wrath.* Ford gave modern America a picture of the Old West that they could hold in their minds forever," she says. "If it weren't for him, that West would largely have disappeared. Now it lives. You can get it on Netflix."

Although Noonan didn't arrive in Massapequa until 1950, World War II definitely dominated her emotional landscape, thanks to the movies. She liked them all, even though "I can't remember a single title, but the actor William Bendix sure was in some of them!" Noonan does, however, recall the plot, which apparently never varied: "The platoon is composed of the Brooklyn wiseguy and the farm boy and the mild-mannered midwestern teacher and the army lifer and the angry young kid. These movies gave me a certain vision of America, or an imprinting of a certain vision, of our differentness and sameness and broad stretch, that never left."

Lest anyone get the impression that Noonan favors nothing but an MGM (circa Louis B. Mayer) view of America, sinister black-and-white clouds occasionally do drift across her otherwise Technicolor dreamscape. "*On the Waterfront,* Elia Kazan's masterpiece,

Sweet Smell of Success
Tony Curtis, 1957

is the most stirring depiction of human courage, the story of a man who wasn't always brave and then willed himself to courage. It made a great impression on me," she says. "And it had a very great score, by Leonard Bernstein. I play it at home as I work."

Regarding her own profession, journalism, she picks *Sweet Smell of Success,* as an influence, capturing as it does "the darkness in the world of Walter Winchell" with its "great script" by Clifford Odets. "And, of course, Orson Welles's *Citizen Kane,* because it captures what is behind all journalism, which is hunger."

And for sheer inspiration at her computer keyboard, there is Robert Bolt: "What a great writer! *Lawrence of Arabia, A Man for All Seasons, Doctor Zhivago*—when I watch those movies, I find I know whole sections of dialogue, pages of it. He gave me a sense of

Boogie Nights
Julianne Moore and Mark Wahlberg, 1997

the sound of words on film. When people laud David Lean (rightly) I always add, 'And Robert Bolt!' "

Noonan has made a career writing about Washington, D.C., but her quick surmise of movies from the past thirty years hints at a possible second act, as a film reviewer:

"I am not sure the work of the director Billy Friedkin has fully received the honor it should: *The Exorcist,* a masterpiece of fear; *The French Connection,* a masterpiece of anxiety.

"*The Godfather: Parts I and II,* has given us not only phrases that entered the language but, in a way, a certain rough philosophy, and iconic characters so enduring that to this day if you say, 'He's a Sonny, not a Michael,' or, 'He's Fredo,' people know exactly what you're saying.

"Paul Thomas Anderson, he's a real artist. *Boogie Nights* is a masterpiece with an unfortunate name. No one ever captured the 1970s like that, when decadence was innocent.

"We await a masterpiece of modern politics."

Bill Maher *Host,* Real Time with Bill Maher

For satirist Bill Maher, the movies have always been about sex and politics. But mainly they've been about sex, especially when he was a kid. As Maher explains, "You have memories of a movie being good and then when you see it again as an adult, you go, 'That sucks!' But at age twelve you thought it was good because you were looking at Ann-Margret's tits. That's what was guiding your editorial view."

Maher's cinematic horniness most likely found full flower early, with Billy Wilder's classic *Some Like It Hot.* Unlike his dedication to Ann-Margret, however, he very rarely genuflected at the altar of Marilyn Monroe. "I didn't like her look that much," he recalls. "But in *Some Like It Hot,* she was super hot. I vividly remember watching it with my mother and sister at home on TV and the second the movie was over I announced that I had to go to bed, and I raced up to my room to masturbate. The film ended at 11 P.M. And I came at 11:01 P.M." For the young Maher, the climactic moment of the film arrived when Monroe makes out with Tony Curtis, who pretends to be impotent. "He's in his Cary Grant mode. With that long kiss I could feel my boner rising," he says. "On top of that, it's funny."

Maher also appreciates the nearly see-through gown that Orry-Kelly created for Monroe's big number, "I Wanna Be Loved by You."

"That moment in the film reminds me of when she sang 'Happy Birthday' to Kennedy," he notes. "It was that same sort of spangly body suit that she just poured herself into. It was really inappropriate, wildly inappropriate. Did nobody say to her before-hand, 'You're going to sing to the president in *that*? Get rid of the tits suit. You're not blowing Kennedy!'"

Post–*Some Like It Hot,* Maher's passion for movies included a few really bad ones starring Ann-Margret: "If you could catch some of her cleavage at twelve or thirteen years old, that's what you lived for." Elke Sommer in the 1966 Hollywood potboiler *The Oscar* also hit the spot: "I didn't care about the movie, but she was hot rolling around in this big bed with Stephen Boyd."

And equally memorable was Yvette Mimieux in a spring-break epic from 1960: "That's another girl I had a hard-on for. In *Where the Boys Are,* she is crossing the highway and gets hit by a car, because the girl who fucks has to be killed. Cut down like a slaughtered pig!"

Not that Maher is one to knock sexual repression in the movies. "Oh, it makes you sexier and hornier in a way. I'm glad there wasn't porn when I was a kid. I don't know what it does to a young mind to see a Tasmanian bucket-fuck when you're only ten years old. A little cleavage should be enough at that age."

What the movies taught the young Maher about scoring with girls, unfortunately, had to be unlearned immediately. "In *Where the Boys Are,* George Hamilton is the ultimate operator, and I thought he was the coolest thing," he recalls. "He sits down next to a girl at the beach and draws a question mark in the sand. She tells him her name. Then he draws another question mark in the sand. And she tells him where she goes to school. And this goes on." Maher could not wait to implement the *WTBA* pick-up technique. "So the next day I go to school with a pad and paper and draw a question mark and give it to this girl, who now thought I was deaf!"

Eventually, it was the movies that introduced Maher to politics, and as his TV shows *Politically Incorrect* and *Real Time With Bill Maher* would lead one to expect, it was rather leftist politics that first inspired him. "I remember seeing *M*A*S*H* when I was fourteen, and it was my first really adult movie," he says of Robert

M*A*S*H
Elliott Gould and Donald Sutherland, 1970

Altman's comedy, set during the Korean War and released during
the Vietnam War.

> It had some swearing, some nudity, and adult themes that
> were antiwar. It was a little over my head and I liked it. I
> sensed watching it that now I was in an adult world. I don't
> know if I had politics when I was fourteen. *M*A*S*H* may
> have shaped them to come. Certainly it was a counterculture
> age. In 1970, we were still living in an idealistic hippie era. I
> was a little young to be manning the barricades, but I saw
> myself as the little brother going, "Can I tag along and bring
> down the government too?" That was the feeling I had
> when I left the theater after seeing *M*A*S*H*.

Dead Poet's Society
Robin Williams, 1989

Frank Luntz *Political Analyst–Pollster*

Imagine: if Frank Luntz had really followed his movie dream, no one would have coined the term "death tax," and Newt Gingrich might never have been speaker of the House, nor would Rudi Giuliani been elected mayor of New York City.

The political strategist was teaching at the University of Pennsylvania in 1989 when he first saw Peter Weir's *Dead Poet's Society,* the movie that changed his life.

"It was right before the Contract with America, and I had an interest in leaving politics and teaching full time. *Dead Poet's Society* had a huge impact on me," says Luntz, who closely identified with Robin Williams's professor character in the film. "I had the same kind of good relationship with my students. We used to go drinking and gather in the evenings to talk politics and philosophy."

But the movie's ending bummed Luntz, and might have led him away from teaching. In the final reel, one of the students kills himself, and the boy's father falsely accuses Williams of putting crazy ideas in the kids' heads. The students buckle under pressure to rat out their dedicated teacher. "I get emotional talking about it," says Luntz, who wanted the students in *Dead Poet's Society* to stand up for their principles "no matter whatever the pressure." He points to a major precedent for such youthful action: "If you go to the graves in Hungary from the 1956 uprising, they are fifteen- and sixteen-year-old kids. They died for their beliefs."

Luntz ultimately left teaching. "My candidates did too well," he explains, referring to Giuliani and Gingrich, as well as Ross Perot. But years later, he got to meet the *Dead Poet's Society* screenwriter, Tom Schulman, and questioned the Oscar-winning scribe about the movie's ending. For what it was worth, Luntz took deep pleasure in giving Schulman his alternate upbeat finale.

"There are movies I like better, but none has had that kind of emotional appeal. I cried," says Luntz, who is now a Fox News contributor. "In my basement, I still have a six-foot cutout [of Robin Williams] that appeared in all the theaters. I went out and got it even though I was upset by the film's ending. Education is boring. It is awful. I always tried to do what Robin Williams did in that film—make it entertaining and provocative."

Perez Hilton *Gossip Blogger*

By his own always reliable account, Mario Armando Lavandeira Jr. counts nearly 9 million hits to his website perezhilton.com on an average day of dish, making him the Cindy Adams of the bloggosphere. So why le nom de blog?

"When I first started, I used my real name and got death threats," says the Miami native, who now lives in Los Angeles. "I came to Perez Hilton because of the juxtaposition of Perez, the Latino outsider, and Hilton, the mainstream of Hollywood pop culture. The outsider, who is me, infiltrates mainstream Hollywood and offers the outsider perspective on things."

Whatever. His is a slant on celeb life that features rude doodles scrawled across paparazzi photos and a penchant for outing in-the-closet stars.

Lavandeira continues to hone his outré status on the John Cameron Mitchell movies *Short Bus* and *Hedwig and the Angry Inch,* but reserves the "my favorite movie of all time" rank for the 1971 Roald Dahl screen adaptation of *Willy Wonka and the Chocolate Factory,* which predates this blogger's birth by about seven years.

"I could really relate to both Wonka and Charlie," says Lavandeira. "In many ways, Wonka is misunderstood and people have the wrong conceptions of him. And what's weird about the film, too, is that it's almost a love story. If the young Charlie were a thirty-year-old woman, it could work as a love story. But he's an adolescent boy."

No doubt, Lavanderia would like to doodle on *Willy Wonka,* too. In addition to its gay subtext, he fancies Gene Wilder's performance ("career-defining") and the super-fantastical sets: "I was a fat kid growing up. I would have loved to just lick the wallpaper in *Willy Wonka.* My favorite thing is the river of hot chocolate. How great would that have been?"

Lavanderia revisits *Willy Wonka* often, and calls it a great film, because "it transcends the genre. The experience of filming-viewing is a very passive one, unlike the theater or going to see a concert. It's not live. You sit there and watch. But a really good movie engages and makes you feel you're experiencing it in real time."

Willy Wonka is just one film that "made me want to immerse myself in the world of entertainment and imagination," says

Moulin Rouge
Nicole Kidman and Ewan McGregor, 2001

Lavanderia. Another is *Moulin Rouge.* "Once again, I felt like I was going to see a live musical. It's so rare that people spontaneously burst into applause at the movies, and that happened repeatedly throughout *Moulin Rouge.* No one could have made *Moulin Rouge* but Baz Luhrmann."

But it's not all chocolate factories and risqué night clubs for this gossip hound. Lavanderia also deeply relates to the loss of family in Robert Zemeckis's *Contact* ("the Jodie Foster character has lost a parent at an early age") and Paul Thomas Anderson's *Magnolia* ("Tom Cruise is estranged from his father, Jason Robards").

"I had an out-of-body experience while watching those films," he says. "They seem real. My dad passed way when I was twelve. I loved him very much. Now my mom lives with me. I moved her up from Miami with my sister, and we're all together again."

Larry King *Host,* Larry King Live

For little Lawrence Harvey Zeiger, his introduction to the movies was not a pleasant one: "I was three. There was a night scene with a guy on a motorcycle coming right at you, so I ran out of the theater."

Today, Zeiger, a.k.a. Larry King, doesn't remember the movie, except that it starred George Raft and "it scared me to death."

Moviegoing proved less stressful in the coming years despite nights haunted by images from *King Kong* ("that gorilla on the Empire State Building") and *Gunga Din* ("climbing up the hill with Cary Grant"). Disney's 1940 animated feature *Pinocchio* left a rosier afterglow, especially its Oscar-winning song, "When You Wish Upon a Star." (In time, King would sing it to his daughter, Kelly: "And when I took her to the movies to see *Pinocchio* when she was four and Jiminy Crickett sang, she jumped up and said, 'Daddy, they're playing our song!'")

The movies' biggest impact came from a series of antiwar films, starting with William Wyler's 1946 Oscar winner, *The Best Years of Our Lives,* in which Harold Russell, a real-life World War II soldier and double amputee, played a veteran returning home from the battlefield. "The film made me antiwar," says King, "because it dealt with the problems of vets getting jobs and how the community treated them. Later, I could relate it to the Vietnam vets. War is stupid."

Back in the early 1970s, when King was doing TV and radio interviews from Miami, "I didn't take a stand on things. I still don't," he says. But the experience of seeing *The Best Years of Our Lives, Paths of Glory,* and *Dr. Strangelove* and reading David Halberstam's Vietnam War treatise *The Best and the Brightest* "taught me not to think that the people in government are smarter than me."

King adds *Full Metal Jacket* to Stanley Kubrick's impressive triptych of antiwar films *Paths of Glory* and *Dr. Strangelove.* The master director's *2001: A Space Odyssey,* however, speaks to him in another way. "I'm not crazy about computers, and that was an

2001: A Space Odyssey
Keir Dullea, 1968

anti-computer movie," insists. "HAL, the computer, not obeying in-structions? He takes them to a place they didn't want to go!"

King doesn't go so far as his fellow septuagenarian John Mc-Cain and claim to have no knowledge of operating a computer. "I can sit down and use one," says the host of CNN's highest-rated show. "I can't tell you the last time I used one. I have assistants. Same thing with BlackBerrys. I don't have a BlackBerry. The assis-tants have BlackBerrys. I don't want some thing to own me. I salute John McCain on that."

Arianna Huffington *Editor in Chief,* Huffington Post

Arianna Stassinopolis was known as a true liberal after graduating from Cambridge University in the early 1970s. Her conversion to conservatism in the 1980s preceded her marriage to oil millionaire Michael Huffington, and shortly after their divorce in 1997, she went back to her liberal roots, founding the leftist *Huffington Post* in 2005. Likewise, her considerable output of books runs the gamut, from biography *(Maria Callas)* to spirituality *(The Fourth Instinct)* to politics *(Right Is Wrong)*.

Politics and print came early to Arianna, thanks to her journalist father and a steady diet of movies imported from Hollywood. "*Mr. Smith Goes to Washington* left quite an impression on me as a young girl growing up in Greece—both for its political message that an impassioned individual can make a big difference in the world, and for its ultimately optimistic depiction of America," she recalls. "I loved how it offered up both a cynical and an idealistic view of government—and while idealism might triumph more often in the movies than in real life, a belief in the ability of good people to make real and lasting change is a belief deeply ingrained in my DNA.

"And *His Girl Friday*—the Cary Grant, Roz Russell, Howard Hawks take on *The Front Page*—appealed to me on so many levels: the excitement of tracking a hot story helped plant the journalism bug in my brain; the incredible verbal dexterity and battles helped inspire my love for a good argument (honed during my time at the Cambridge debating society); and Russell's strong, confident, gifted, star reporter was an incredible example of a powerful woman operating in what has traditionally been a man's world."

Although Hollywood often takes the rap for glamorizing, simplifying, or just plain distorting the work-a-day world, Huffington is able to pick a number of films, beyond the classic *Mr. Smith* and *His Girl Friday,* that portray her professional milieu with accuracy and deft insight:

"*All the President's Men* captures the excitement of investigative journalism, with some of the highest stakes imaginable.

"*Network* and *Ace in the Hole* brilliantly and satirically show the dark forces that can affect the information we get. When *Network* was released [in 1976], it played like over-the-top satire. Watch it now and it feels like a documentary.

"*The Candidate* still holds up. It shows how idealism can give way to realpolitik—and an idealist can be seduced by the lure of power. That moment when Robert Redford, having improbably won, turns to Peter Boyle, playing his campaign manager, and asks, 'What do we do now?' is priceless."

Huffington ought to know: in 1994 she campaigned unsuccessfully for Mr. Huffington's bid to be a U.S. senator, and in 2003 she ran unsuccessfully against Arnold Schwarzenegger to be governor of California.

Today, Huffington calls herself a big proponent of the power of political satire, the kind of humor intended to produce not just laughs but change. Or, as she puts it, "Satire in the tradition of Jonathan Swift: savage wit at the service of passionate conviction." On that score, she offers a long list of films, beginning with Stanley Kubrick's *Dr. Strangelove,* which had "a huge impact," she says. "It's a film that close to forty-five years after its release still resonates." In 2008 she even wrote a blog post attacking John McCain's ardor for war, in which Huffington opined, "although he'd be the oldest person ever elected president, McCain doesn't need Viagra—he's got Iraq." She went on to compare McCain to Gen. Buck Turgidson, George C. Scott's war-loving character in *Dr. Strangelove:* "I'm not saying we wouldn't get our hair mussed, but I do say no more than 10 to 20 million killed—tops!"

Other antiwar films have also deeply impressed and affected Huffington:

"*M*A*S*H* stuck a dagger—actually a scalpel—through the notion of war as a romantic endeavor, a painful reality made devastatingly clear in films like *Coming Home, The Deer Hunter, Platoon,* and *Born on the Fourth of July.*

"And, who knows, we might have been able to avoid the nightmare in Iraq if, before voting on the authorization to use military force, every member of Congress had watched David O. Russell's *Three Kings.* Especially if they'd made it a double feature and screened *Gallipoli* as well.

"And I think that with *War, Inc.,* John Cusack has pulled off the near-impossible—finding a savage, reality-altering humor amidst the tragedy of Iraq. It's the rare film that makes you laugh, wince, and become outraged all at the same time."

14

THE FUTURISTS
AND THE FANTASISTS

"Singin' in the Rain is a great science-fiction musical . . .
because it is about the invention of sound and how
that invention changed the history of Hollywood."
—Ray Bradbury

Dr. Neil deGrasse Tyson *Director, Hayden Planetarium*

As chance or destiny would have it, Neil deGrasse Tyson was born
the same week in 1958 that NASA launched. Today, he heads up the
Hayden Planetarium at the American Museum of Natural History, he hosts *NOVA,* and he has authored several best-selling science tomes, including *Just Visiting This Planet* and *Death by Black
Hole*. And so naturally his "favorite film of all time" must be *All
That Jazz*.

"It is so high-cholesterol," Tyson says of Bob Fosse's autobiographical musical from 1979. "I never have seen tragedy surrounded by singing and dancing that one normally performs when
you are happy. That juxtaposition wiped me clean. I couldn't get
out of the chair at the film's end."

In *All That Jazz,* Roy Scheider plays a womanizing, drug-abusing director whose ambitions push him to a fatal heart attack,
which the real-life, hard-living Fosse was able to stave off until age
sixty in 1987. Tyson saw the film when, taking time from his college physics studies, he performed in several dance competitions.
He was, in fact, "wearing leg warmers when I saw the film. I

wanted to cheer the film's song and dance, yet simultaneously I'm brought down by this man's slow death in the film."

Tyson also draws unlikely inspiration, for an astrophysicist, from another tuner: George Cukor's 1964 screen adaptation of *My Fair Lady*. "I have an alter ego," he explains. "If I had another life I'd be a songwriter for corny Broadway musicals, I swear. I like the simple turn of phrase that uses words in clever ways to convey emotions and plotline. When I write essays and my books, I have this goal that there is the perfect phrase I've composed that sits mellifluously on the ears of the reader. They hear the flows of words in their minds. *My Fair Lady* is the apogee of this other identity I have. I watch it a couple of times a year."

In Tyson's pantheon of films, Stanley Kubrick's *2001: A Space Odyssey* rests closer to his planetarium home. "It is the most influential in terms of carving, shaping, and guiding a personal vision. It is the beginning of the end of the future that never came. . . . Tomorrowland."

Tyson dissects those late 1950s and early 1960s newspaper articles that depict how the future would look in the 1970s and the 1980s. "You don't see those anymore," he points out. "*2001* was the last great dream about the future in terms of a realistic, tangible future: the clean spaceships, the silence of space only punctuated by classical music, the corporations in space like Howard Johnson's. That was the last hurrah. I didn't know it was the last hurrah at the time. The movie since then has grown in significance."

Blade Runner is another sci-fi film that Tyson admires more today than when he first saw it in 1982. If *2001* represented the end of optimism, Ridley Scott's movie signaled the beginning of our overriding dread of the future. But Tyson insists he's no pessimist.

"What people forget is that we're not without control over the decline of our society," he observes. "Nothing ever gets as bad as the apocalyptic people say it will. There is a restoring force that brings it back to the middle. And nothing ever gets as utopian as

Blade Runner
Harrison Ford, 1982

people suggest. People are not that visionary. We're somewhere in the middle, disappointingly so."

If there's any film that perfectly melds Tyson's love of science and showbiz, it's *Happy Feet,* the 2006 Oscar winner for animated feature, about a tap-dancing penguin. "From its opening scene, you come at Earth from space and the Earth rotates so Antarctica is at the top of the world. From the beginning it establishes a point of view, and you are in the culture of the penguins whose food supply is disappearing, and they have to pray to the food gods. But one penguin is curious and finds out what's going on. You can never be wise and stay in your hometown. This movie is not your happy animal thing. It is deep," Tyson claims.

Happy Feet
2006

Overall, Tyson believes that the movies have greatly affected his life. "I read few novels. I read nonfiction. And movies are a fundamental source of my exposure to the interactions between people in different places and different cultures and different times. Films over the years have enabled me to remain more socialized as a scientist," says the astrophysicist on Central Park West.

Brad Bird *Animated Filmmaker*

Because Brad Bird is writer-director of three of the most acclaimed animated films of recent years—*The Iron Giant, The Incredibles,* and *Ratatouille*—it's no surprise to hear him extol the virtues both of Warner Brothers toon legend Michael Maltese and *Lawrence of Arabia* scribe Robert Bolt.

Bird, whose own name appears on that shortest of short lists, that of writers who were Oscar-nominated for their screenwriting on animated features (for *Incredibles*), combines the whimsical genius of Maltese and lofty ambition of Bolt in *Ratatouille*. He chafes, however, at any discussion of animation writing that doesn't make clear his belief that "good writing is good writing. The whole question of writing for animation is skewed," says Bird. "There isn't a giant difference between animation and live action. You need characters, stories, themes. It's called good storytelling."

Bird feels misconceptions about the writing of animated features emanate from both sides of the fence—from those who can't imagine serious work from the makers of cartoons and from those inside the animated field who can't imagine that any writer who doesn't begin as an animator can ever fully embrace the medium.

Bird explains that although he did begin his career in animation, "I write scripts first, before the work gets to the storyboarding stage. But I write with the knowledge of what animation can do."

Once Bird has made clear that in his view there are no lines separating genres, he expands on the artists who have influenced him in both the animation and live-action camps. From the Disney canon, Bird cites *Lady and the Tramp* and *Pinocchio* as examples of storytelling with "strong story beats and well-delineated characters." He also admires Nick Park of *Wallace and Grommit* fame as "an artist with a singular point of view" and *My Neighbor Totoro*'s Hayao Miyazaki as "a master of great storytelling."

And then there are his fellow artists at Pixar, which he calls the home team. "*Toy Story*'s power comes from its talking about death under several layers of action," says Bird, who sees the film's real message as "Do you use your life or do you prolong it and become entombed?"

For Bird, Maltese is "the king of the Warner Brothers shorts" and he says that "95 percent of the finest days in the Chuck Jones career had Maltese attached."

On the live-action writing front, Bird rhapsodizes about Bolt's *Lawrence of Arabia* script; it's a movie he recalls seeing as a youth and, "Though I didn't understand it, it overwhelmed me. It told me the world was a much more complex place than I ever imagined."

Brad reserves a special place in his pantheon of film talents for one of the directing greats: "Alfred Hitchcock is the one who taught me that there are people making these movies. I kept seeing these movies that gave me chills," Bird says of everything from *Shadow of a Doubt* to *Psycho,* "and I kept seeing his name. I thought, 'Aha, it's the same guy giving me these chills. And his name is Alfred Hitchcock.' "

Jeff Smith *Comics Creator*

"Animation looks the way I dream," says Jeff Smith, creator of the epic *Bone* comic series, which is well into its second decade. "There's something about the way it's flattened out, the way things move that looks like the kinds of images you have in your head when you're daydreaming. It really brings things that are unbelievable to life."

For Smith, the two animation masters who best capture the artistic potential of the medium are Walt Disney and Hayao Miyazaki. He saw his first Disney cartoon when he was four or five years old. *Snow White and the Seven Dwarfs,* he says, really couldn't have been made any other way: "There's no other medium that could have had these completely unrealistic cartoon characters interacting with a human."

Disney's dreamlike imagination, evidenced by such surreal touches as talking animals, continued even after Walt's death with projects like *The Lion King,* another Smith favorite.

"Interestingly enough, that's the only Disney film that has no time frame, it has no humans," he says. "Even *Bambi,* where you never see a human being, there are gunshots heard and you can see a camp, so there's some sense that it's in modern times. With *The Lion King,* that whole Circle of Life thing could take place at any time."

It was actually the *Heavy Metal* comics series, not animated movies, that set Smith's imagination free during the 1970s; the live-

My Neighbor Totoro
1988

action *Jaws* and *Star Wars* unlocked further possibilities. "I was really excited by some of the visual storytelling I was seeing," he says.

Smith felt similar admiration in the mid-1990s when he discovered Miyazaki's work: "I'd been doing *Bone* for about four years when I saw *My Neighbor Totoro,* and it kind of blew my mind." Here was a story about being a child that seamlessly incorporated elements of fantasy, featuring a benevolent forest spirit who befriends two young girls.

"I just don't know how Miyazaki managed to put so many ideas, so many concepts and emotions into such a short movie. And yet, he still took the time to quietly look at scenery. There's all these quiet moments in *Totoro* where you're looking at clouds going past a tree or pollywogs swimming in a creek, and that's astonishing to me," says Smith.

That same attention to detail impressed him in the 2006 Disney feature *Open Season*. "Artistically, it was probably the most accomplished computer-animated film to date," he says. "They did things graphically that reach back to Disney's heyday in the

1940s and 1950s, really stunning vistas and what looked like two-dimensional graphics, but then would move."

Smith likes all types of movies, but he insists the best films feature plenty of humor.

"Chaplin to me is the perfect visual artist," he says. "He made things funny by making them human, and I think the same thing about Disney and Miyazaki: when you laugh in those movies, it's because you recognize yourself completely. My own sense of humor in *Bone* is all based on embarrassment and chaos; I think those are the two funniest things in the world."

Dr. Leonard Susskind *Physicist*

Leonard Susskind, a founder of string theory and author of *The Cosmic Landscape,* is not a huge fan of science fiction—and for good reason. "Science to me is sufficiently weird and interesting, and stranger than fiction," says this Stanford University professor. One sci-fi classic and one rather cheesy horror film, however, did impress him as a child and young adult.

"I liked reading Jules Verne, and the movie *20,000 Leagues Under the Sea* caught my fascination," Susskind says of the 1954 Disney film. "It was visually very good, and the Captain Nemo [James Mason] was exactly as I pictured him from the Jules Verne story. But did it make me want to be a scientist?" Probably not. "I didn't learn anything about science until I was twenty. I was already well into college, and I had no idea I wanted to be a scientist or what science was about. But exploring the unknown world of the ocean appealed to me. Exploring the unknown is a part of every scientist's life. The unknown I explore now, however, is not something that can be portrayed well on the movie screen."

One B-grade horror film proved somewhat more key to Susskind's future career. He retells the movie epiphany: "I was five years old and we lived in the South Bronx; we were poor street urchins and lived on the street. My friends were a little older than me; they were eight. We saw *Abbott and Costello Meet Frankenstein* [in 1948], and I was so scared when Lou Costello sat himself down in the lap of the Monster. Not realizing where he was, Costello's face dropped and he got more and more frightened. I was so scared. My friends teased me and played monster. My goal was to become a mad scientist and get back at them. And here I am, mad as hell!"

Although it's a spoof, *Abbott and Costello Meet Frankenstein* stars two giants of the horror genre: Lon Chaney Jr. played the Wolf Man and Bela Lugosi did his usual bit as Count Dracula. Boris Karloff, however, had forsaken his Frankenstein Monster, and for much of the 1940s, he left that signature role to the aptly named and very large Glenn Strange, who played Mary Shelley's creature in the Abbott and Costello movie as well as *House of Frankenstein* and *House of Dracula*.

Fortunately, Susskind recovered from his encounter with Mr. Strange, and wrote *The Black Hole War* (2008), about his longstanding argument with Stephen Hawking and how it was resolved, among many other weird and interesting things.

Alan Weisman *Author*

In his 2007 best-seller, *The World Without Us,* Alan Weisman speculates on just such a scenario—Earth sans man. As he predicts it, within two weeks of the last man walking in Manhattan, the city's subways will already be filled with water. Within the year, all nuclear plants will melt down. And after a hundred millennia, the planet will finally return to pre-human levels of carbon dioxide.

Weisman obviously harbors a fascination with the apocalyptic, and that interest is one he can trace back to the movies. "When I started writing this book, there's one movie that I vividly recalled seeing as a child," he says. "*On the Beach* had a huge impact on me, and I screened it again while writing *The World Without Us.*"

In Stanley Kramer's 1959 movie, based on the sci-fi best-seller by Nevil Shute, Australia is the last continent inhabited by man after the rest of the world has been decimated by a nuclear war. But time is running out in the land of Oz, and it is the film's recurring image of a street banner in Melbourne—"There Is Still Time . . . Brother"—that haunted Weisman for decades.

"In the beginning, there's an evangelist preacher in front of a huge crowd; then later, there's a third of the people left, and in the last scene we see only the banner and no one is left in the street," he notes.

Influential movies aren't necessarily classic movies, as Weisman points out with regard to *On the Beach*. "Gregory Peck is not one of the great actors of his generation, and some of the dialogue in Stanley Kramer's movie is hokey," he offers. "And yet the emotional heart of *On the Beach* is in the right place and it comes through beautifully: we are capable of going too far."

In the early 1990s, Weisman worked on the National Public Radio series *Vanishing Homelands* and visited Punta Arenas, Chile, the southernmost city in the world, where an ozone hole had opened in the sky and parents watched as their children were suddenly at risk for skin cancer for the very first time. "We didn't do this," they told Weisman. "The damage is coming to us."

"They had never seen sunburns before," he recalls. "I burst into tears. That experience had an echo of *On the Beach*."

Weisman finds the world beset by overpopulation, and that concern surfaces in two other movies that have affected his social conscience.

"*Soylent Green* is set in 2020, and the gist is that there are so many people that we've eaten ourselves out of house and planet," he says of the Charlton Heston movie, directed by Richard Fleischer in 1973.

Weisman finds the polyglot culture in *Blade Runner* especially "fascinating. We're moving toward that," he says. Other aspects of Ridley Scott's sci-fi film, however, alarm him. "The sheer number of people is terrifying. We're headed toward 9 billion by midcentury. We're growing a million every four days; that's clearly not a sustainable level of growth."

KAWS *Graffiti Artist*

First came advertising, then came KAWS, the New York–based graffiti artist also known as Brian Donnelly, who literally "defaced" phone-booth and bus-shelter fashion ads by DKNY, Calvin Klein, and others by painting his trademark skull-and-crossbones over the models' mugs.

The skull made its way onto Mickey Mouse's body, then the Simpsons. In 2006, KAWS opened his Original Fake store in Tokyo, and he says he purposefully targeted the animated characters because of their international appeal: "I love how they're so integrated into people's lives. Even in Japan, you go 'D'oh,' and people know what you're doing. You can't really name off politicians or other people who are recognized like that."

Though KAWS's work references animation, he says it's the cartoons' iconography, not their stories, that appeal to him. "One of the first VHS tapes I ever bought when I was like fifteen was *Akira,* and I watched that over and over," he says of Katsuhiro Otomo's 1988 film, which envisions a plot to destroy the city of Tokyo. "At that age, to even lay down the money for that was a big thing for me. The drawing was just amazing, all the switches of perspective."

Regarding sci-fi or horror stories with real actors, KAWS found that Jake Gyllenhaal's bouts with a large bunny in Richard Kelly's *Donnie Darko* "kinda shook me up." KAWS saw it twice in theaters—that hardly ever happens, he says—and inspired his *Accomplice* character, a pink rabbit toy he made soon after. *Donnie Darko* opened in New York City on October 28, 2001. "I think it might have been one of the first times out of my apartment after 9/11, so the whole vibe of everything was sort of off. It was surreal,

Donnie Darko
Jake Gyllenhaal, 2001

like the giant plane engine crashing through the house—just the timing, something about that movie hit the right spot," he says with appropriately spooked-out enthusiasm.

Beyond those celluloid thrills, KAWS confesses a short attention span. Not many movies impress him, he says, although he has a soft spot for documentaries about other artists, like Roy Lichtenstein and R. Crumb. Terry Zwigoff's *Crumb* from 1994 especially resonates. "I just thought it was such a great inside look into this artist's world, panning across all these little intimate things on his shelf," he says.

Frank Cho *Comics Creator*

Liberty Meadows creator Frank Cho was born in Seoul, South Korea, and came to the United States "the same year Norman Rock-

Finding Nemo
2003

well died, so his art was all over newspapers and magazines," says the self-taught comics illustrator. Cho credits Rockwell with influencing him to become an artist, but he also confesses a weakness for Tex Avery cartoons.

When it comes to animated movies, Cho's favorites are of a more recent vintage. He loves the retro-styled robot movie *The Iron Giant* (1999), directed by Brad Bird, and thinks Pixar's *Finding Nemo* (2003) is tops.

"It's an emotionally heavy story, if you think about it," he says of *Nemo*. "In the opening sequence, the guy loses his wife and all of his kids. Being a parent, I guess that struck a chord with me."

Lately, Cho has been drawing Marvel's popular superhero series *The Mighty Avengers*. "It's only in the last five years or so I thought that the technology has caught up to the point where Hollywood could do a really great superhero movie," he says. "I think the best superhero movie so far is *The Incredibles*," he says, referring to another Bird-directed movie. "I think Pixar really nailed it."

But the movies that most directly connect to Cho's work are all live action, he says. Cho has lost count of how many times he has seen Frank Darabont's 1994 prison feature, *The Shawshank Redemption.* "I watch it over and over again, trying to figure out how to tell a character-driven story that is also plot-driven," he says. "There's no fat around the story."

Anne Rice *Novelist*

Anne Rice's career easily breaks into two phases: her early Undead period and her late Christian period. Likewise, Rice's moviegoing habits reflect a similar split.

First came the blood and fangs by way of Lambert Hillyer's *Dracula's Daughter,* made in 1936. "It's an old black-and-white film of great ambiance and subtlety, and I saw it as a child, and it established the myth of the vampire for me," says Rice. "It has some of the best vampire scenes I've ever seen on film. They've never been surpassed."

Not that she thinks Neil Jordan's 1994 screen adaptation of her *Interview With the Vampire* novel is any piker in its casting of Tom Cruise and Brad Pitt as bloodsuckers. "In its own way, it made history," she says. "It's a unique film in the way that *The Red Shoes* is unique. [Producer] David Geffen really went all the way with it."

As for the blood and thorns, Rice's interest in religion has only recently been rekindled. Raised in the Roman Catholic Church, she called herself an atheist for most of her adult life, then, in 1996, returned to the church and has begun to write novels like *Christ the Lord, Out of Egypt.*

Again, it was a movie, *Quo Vadis,* that first got her hooked on the subject of religion. "The film had just about everything a young kid would want in the way of exotic banquet and palace scenes, and deep moral discussions of what the Christian message means," she says. "I will never forget the grand depiction of ancient Rome, of the handsome hero Marcus [Robert Taylor] falling in love with the beautiful Christian Lygia [Deborah Kerr]. There was also the struggle of the persecuted and peace-loving Christians against the corrupt emperor [Peter Ustinov]; yet, it was wondrously entertaining with fabulous action scenes, such as the Christians fleeing from the horrendous fire that Nero started to burn down Rome."

But the class-act of religious films for Rice remains Fred Zinnemann's *The Nun's Story,* released in 1959 and starring Audrey Hepburn. "It beautifully depicted the struggle of a young woman to give her life entirely to God as a nun. I have watched this film countless times. It is my hands-down favorite religious film," says Rice, who also speaks of the "powerful" and "transformative effect" of *The Robe, Ben-Hur, The Passion of the Christ,* and other Christian-themed movies. She unabashedly loves the genre. "I was affected as much by *Quo Vadis,* about wanting to be a Christian, as I have been by Robert Bresson's *Diary of a Country Priest,* about how hard the road to Christ can be," she says.

Ray Bradbury *Novelist*

He's the giant of the genre, and so it means something when Ray Bradbury says, "My favorite science-fiction movie is *Close Encounters of the Third Kind* because it's philosophical, it's religious. It fits together pieces of the universe."

Never at a loss to explain what he means, the author of *Fahrenheit 451* continues at rapid-fire speed: "If you look at the Sistine Chapel ceiling, God reaches down through space to touch the hand of Adam, and Adam has his hand out toward God and the contact is made. That is the great thing about Steven Spielberg's film: we are in touch with another part of the universe, and the two halves

Close Encounters of the Third Kind
1977

of the universe are connected. You come out of that movie changed. It is one of the greatest movie experiences I've ever had."

Bradbury unabashedly loves movies, and he claims that they have had a major impact on his life, especially the films of Lon Chaney. When Bradbury talks about those silent pictures, it's as if they unspooled yesterday for the first time: "I was three when I saw Chaney's *The Hunchback of Notre Dame* [1923]; at four I saw his *He Who Gets Slapped* [1924], and at five I saw his *The Phantom of the Opera* [1925]. They inspired me."

If they were the genesis of his imagination, then it was the original *Lost World* (1925) and *King Kong* (1933) that kicked off Bradbury's love for dinosaurs, which in turn brought him to the movies as a screenwriter.

"I wrote a dinosaur story, *The Foghorn,* and because John Huston read that book, he hired me to write the screenplay for *Moby*

Dick. It's incredible: the dinosaurs I saw in the movies changed my life."

Before Bradbury scripted Huston's 1956 film, with an improbably cast Gregory Peck as Captain Ahab, he became a huge fan of *Singin' in the Rain,* which he calls a "great science-fiction musical." How so? "It is science-fiction because it is about the invention of sound and how that invention changed the history of Hollywood."

Bradbury became so psyched by Stanley Donen's and Gene Kelly's 1952 tuner that he wanted to write the dancer-actor-director a movie, and offered Kelly his short story "The Black Ferris." Unfortunately, Kelly couldn't get the money to finance the film, so Bradbury expanded his tale about an evil carnival's effect on small-town America into the classic fantasy novel *Something Wicked This Way Comes,* which eventually did make it to the screen.

"It's beautiful," Bradbury says of Jack Clayton's 1983 film version. "It follows my book and my screenplay closely."

THE HISTORIANS

"The romance of the Civil War was set by *Gone With the Wind,* which makes slavery into something positive. People still romance that war. No other film had that effect on me."
—*Doris Kearns Goodwin*

Tom Brokaw *TV Journalist, NBC*

The erstwhile NBC anchor is partial to his home state of South Dakota. Tom Brokaw proudly hails from the town of Webster; his paternal great-grandfather founded Bristol, S.D.; and as he points out, nearby Omaha produced such movie greats as Marlon Brando, Henry Fonda, and Fred Astaire.

"What was it in the Missouri River water of that otherwise conventional midsize city that turned out such luminescent talent?" he asks.

Brando figures especially huge in Brokaw's youth. "When I was thirteen I broke a foot playing basketball, so the local theater owner took pity and hired me as the popcorn vender," he says, thinking back to 1953. "When *The Wild One* came to our theater, I was so transfixed by the action on the screen I burned three batches of popcorn, and my career was over before it started."

Post-popcorn and his NBC anchor days, Brokaw wrote the book *Boom! Voices of the Sixties: Personal Reflections on the '60s and Today.* On that topic, he champions *The Graduate* as the decade's most influential movie: "Because it signaled a generational shift in

The Graduate
Dustin Hoffman, 1967

attitudes about life, careers, sex, and personal choices. Moreover, Mike Nichols took the art of filmmaking to a brilliant new level with his direction."

Brokaw's personal picks of motion pictures very much reflect his professional life. "I am not sure any film said to me, 'A-ha, journalism! Why didn't I think of that before?'" he cautions. But a few films nonetheless had their effect on him. "*His Girl Friday* with Roz Russell and Cary Grant was, for me, a working-class kid in a conservative, small prairie town, a tantalizing taste of what life could be like," he says of Howard Hawks's 1940 film, based on the Ben Hecht and Charles MacArthur play *The Front Page*. "Their sassy ways and snappy dialogue were so seductive I wanted to be a part of that. I later came to know both Cary and Roz, and they were even more appealing in real life."

He unequivocally calls *All the President's Men* "the best film about journalism ever made. Director Alan J. Pakula, Robert Redford as Bob Woodward, Dustin Hoffman as Carl Bernstein, Jason Robards as Ben Bradlee, and scriptwriter William Goldman gave us an authentic portrayal of the hard work, courage, and terror that come with chasing a big story and getting it right."

Brokaw also admires *Broadcast News,* calling James L. Brooks's 1987 film "a send-up of the vanities of my profession," but one that captures "the almost blood relationship between producer and correspondent, in this case, Holly Hunter and Albert Brooks."

This veteran newsman does broker one caveat with regard to *Broadcast News,* asking, "Why did the big ego, shallow-brained anchor (William Hurt) have to be named Tom? Mr. Brooks (James, that is), why not a Jim?"

Robert A. Caro *Biographer*

Robert A. Caro thinks of his major biography subject, Lyndon Johnson, whenever he watches the scene in *Lawrence of Arabia* where Peter O'Toole lets the match burn his bare fingers and says without flinching, "The trick, William Potter, is not minding it hurts."

"That's an example of really rare willpower. That scene makes me think of Johnson, who showed the same kind of will," says the Pulitzer Prize–winning author of the LBJ biographies *The Path of Power* and *Means of Ascent*. The latter book contains a scene of rare willpower not unlike O'Toole's match trick in the 1962 David Lean film.

"In Johnson's case, he is running for election to the Senate in 1948, his last chance, or his career might well be over," explains Caro. "During the campaign, he develops this kidney stone. It is incredibly painful, and the doctors don't see how he can go on campaigning. He has a fever of over 105 degrees, but he won't stop campaigning and he won't allow the doctors to operate. In those days, an operation to remove a kidney stone required six weeks of immobility, after which he would have no chance to win. Although he is endangering his life, Johnson won't let them operate."

Caro titled the chapter "Will!"

A penchant for "great idealism and a ruthlessness in accomplishing great ends" also link Johnson and *Lawrence*, in Caro's opinion.

And this scribe has other reasons for putting *Lawrence of Arabia* at the very top of his movie bio list. "David Lean seems to feel, as I do, that history in part turns on character, on the personalities of the great figures of an era. In Lyndon Baines Johnson's presidency, his personality has significant weight in affecting history— in civil rights, for example, and in Vietnam. And in *Lawrence of Arabia,* you see how Lawrence's character influences the fate of an entire region. The very creation of the Middle East is affected by his character."

Despite his admiration for Lean's classic, Caro remains underwhelmed by most biopics. "If you're talking about biography, you have to examine character with a depth that is very hard for movies to do. Since character is an interior thing, it is very hard to show it. *Lawrence of Arabia,* in my opinion, is an epic movie that hinges on the character of its hero."

Caro also gives high marks to Stephen Frears's 2006 movie, *The Queen,* but not as a biography of Elizabeth II, played by Helen Mirren in her Oscar-winning turn. "I thought of it as a political movie, not a biography movie. It was a movie about not one but two great politicians," he says.

Especially memorable for Caro is the scene where the queen, speaking on TV to her British subjects, finally expresses her remorse over the death of Princess Diana. And as she's talking, Tony Blair, played by Michael Sheen, tells his wife, "Be quiet! This is how you survive!" According to Caro, "[Blair] is watching intently, it is like he's studying what she's saying. It's not just about one politician, Blair. It is the queen as a great politician also. If she

Lawrence of Arabia
Peter O'Toole, 1962

hadn't made this speech, the movie hints strongly that the British people might have abolished the monarchy. The queen finally takes Tony Blair's advice and gives a perfect political speech."

Lisa Dennison *Executive Vice President, Sotheby's*

When it comes to history and art, the former director of the Guggenheim Museum in New York City isn't overly impressed with Hollywood fare like *The Agony and the Ecstasy,* with Charlton Heston playing Michelangelo, or *Lust for Life,* with Kirk Douglas playing Vincent Van Gogh. "They were too literal for my taste," says Dennison.

Like the museum she once presided over, Dennison goes for the modern. "I think Andy Warhol's *Trash* from 1970 captures the spirit of an era that is vital to the art world as we know it today,"

The Red Balloon
Pascal Lamorisse, 1956

she says. "More recently, I loved Ed Harris's *Pollock*. He vividly re-created some of the seminal figures of America's defining art movement, abstract expressionism."

Dennison also praises a 2007 film by Milos Forman that almost no one else saw in its original first-run release. "*Goya's Ghosts* is a visually sumptuous and deeply moving encounter with Goya and his art," she offers. "From the opening titles through the period-specific set design to the closing credits, you feel as if you are im-mersed in the very pigment of his paintings. I found it a deeply emotional experience, and learned more about the politics of the era and the world of art patronage than I could have imagined a film could expose."

Regarding the movie that may have changed her life, Denni-son points to an Albert Lamorisse film she saw at an especially impressionable age. "A film that had a huge impact on me and the path I would later take was *Le ballon rouge* [*The Red Balloon*] from 1956," says the museum director–turned–auction house executive. "It is about a boy in Paris who finds a balloon that appears to have a life of its own as it leads him through the streets of Paris. It has a surreal and whimsical quality which reminds me of the art of Paul Klee and Jean Miro. Indeed, the greatest painting by Paul Klee in the Guggenheim collection is called *The Red Balloon*. Perhaps my early exposure to this romantic sensibility of the French led me to major in French and art history in college."

Bob Gazzale *President and CEO, American Film Institute*

According to the American Film Institute and its CBS series *AFI 100 Years, Psycho* is the number-one thriller, *Casablanca* is the number-one romance, and *Some Like It Hot* is the number-one comedy. Obviously, the AFI likes numbers. But no way can you get its president and CEO, Bob Gazzale, to choose a personal number-one film in any category. It's not for fear of offending any moviemaker friends.

"There are just too many films to choose from the hundreds of thousands I've seen," he complains.

Regarding first movie impressions, however, Gazzale does remember *The Wizard of Oz* with unabashed fondness. "I used to watch it every year on TV. It doesn't get much better than that," he says.

It's the repeated viewings that get him hooked on a movie: "One of the truly magical aspects of movies is how differently you can respond to the same movie at different points in your life. The true classics stay with you. We see them as a child, and then later we appreciate them in a whole new way."

For example, "I was twelve years old when I saw *Close Encounters of the Third Kind,* and I identified with the kids and their

Vertigo
James Stewart and Kim Novak, 1958

sense of wonderment," he says. "I had seen the 1953 version of *War of the Worlds,* but after seeing *Close Encounters,* I thought, 'Hey, the aliens might be nice people!' Now when I see the film, I am Richard Dreyfuss with the mashed potatoes and his getting on the ship. That is a whole new movie for me now. Ask me about a movie and what influenced me, and I'll have different answers depending on when I saw it."

Gazzale has a special affinity for black-and-white films. "Maybe because they transport me back to my childhood. I'm back to who I was when life was more simple. That's part of what black-and-white does to me chemically."

Younger audiences, he realizes, have a real aversion to any film not shot in color. "They didn't grow up with that TV black-and-white experience," he says. But there is hope, he believes. Gazzale's seven-year-old son has learned to love Marx Brothers movies, even though it took him a while: "When I first introduced him to *Duck Soup*, he asked, 'Daddy, what's wrong with the television?'"

Today, most movies get watched on TV, and that goes triple for repeated viewings. Gazzale mentions two films that, when they pop up inadvertently on the tube, he cannot switch the channels under any circumstances. "There's no chance I'll turn off *The Godfather,*" he says of Francis Ford Coppola's 1972 gangster epic. "There's that opening image of the man's face and the words, 'I believe in America,' and I'm hooked for the next three hours." Another keeper is Alfred Hitchcock's 1958 masterpiece starring James Stewart and Kim Novak. "With *Vertigo,* I get completely lost in that movie," he says. "And it's uncomfortable. It's like being caught in a labyrinth. You're so grateful when the 'The End' appears. You've been on this bizarre, timeless journey with these people. I feel like yelling 'help' halfway through that movie."

Dr. Brent D. Glass *Director, Smithsonian Institution's National Museum of American History*

In his job, Brent D. Glass oversees more than 2 million objects, from the Star Spangled Banner (yes, the one that Francis Scott Key was looking at in the rocket's red glare) to a packet of macrobiotic brown rice. Fondly called "the nation's attic," the museum has not ignored the touchstones of the American film industry. It houses R2-D2 and C-3PO and Indiana Jones's hat and jacket; it's the home of Marilyn Monroe's white kidskin evening gloves and the Alien's egg. Not only does the museum famously display Dorothy's ruby slippers (donated anonymously) and Ray Bolger's tattered scarecrow costume, which the actor kept and used in appearances for years, it has one of the film's original scripts and a Technicolor camera that was used on the *Wizard of Oz* set. "This is an amazing contraption," says the museum's director.

Glass, who would be honored to add National Film Buff to his long list of achievements, seems to have found time to see every

Glory
Jihmi Kennedy, Denzel Washington, and Morgan Freeman, 1989

movie ever made—and more than once. He speaks of them with the encyclopedic recall of a professional movie historian.

"The mission of the National Museum of American History is to tell the story of America. The history of film is a big part of American history, and it's a big part of our collection," says the custodian of all this wonderful stuff. "We have just received from Sylvester Stallone objects from the first and second *Rocky*: his hat, his robe, his gloves, and his shorts. We collect sheet music from composers. We have many Oscars.

"*Glory* is my favorite historical film for a number of reasons," Glass says of Edward Zwick's Civil War feature. "It really brought out a story that was not well known about the service of the 54th Massachusetts Regiment and the whole issue of African Americans serving in the Civil War. It was an important movie. It allowed us to get to the whole question, Why was the Civil War important and why was it fought?

"So often in the past movies have presented a very glamorous and romantic view of the Civil War, overlooking one of its fundamental causes and consequences; the question of slavery and the question of freedom. *Glory* really dramatized the motivation of these young men who wanted to serve and why, of all people, they had a direct self-interest in laying down their lives. That final scene of the charge on Fort Wagner in South Carolina is just an extraordinary battle scene," he adds.

"There were some great performances in there. . . . You had Matthew Broderick, Denzel Washington, and Morgan Freeman," say Glass. "In 1991, RCA Columbia Pictures donated twenty-one objects to the museum that relate to the film, including Morgan Freeman's uniform that he wore when he played Sgt. Maj. John Rawlins and some charcoal sketches and watercolors that were used to create camera angles and scenic compositions in the film."

Glass sat on the advisory commission at Gettysburg Battlefield when the movie *Gettysburg* was made in the early 1990s. "Much of it was filmed at Gettysburg," he recalls. "Martin Sheen plays Gen. Robert E. Lee, and Jeff Daniels plays Col. Joshua Lawrence Chamberlain. To me, it's not as powerful as *Glory,* but it's a good companion movie."

Another movie that the Smithsonian director thinks evokes a period of history effectively is Michael Cimino's 1978 Oscar winner, *The Deer Hunter.* "It's a rich movie with great performances [by] Meryl Streep and Christopher Walken and Robert De Niro. It really captured the feeling of Western Pennsylvania, the steel mill towns, the ethnic influence, and the deer-hunting culture that's very strong throughout the state. There was more than just one way people experienced going through the Vietnam War and the complexity of the times. The movie very effectively conveyed all sorts of individual stories," he continues. "The ending is always so powerful to me when they're sitting around the table singing 'God Bless America.' More recently, after 9/11, it is really moving to see that again in a different context."

At the time Glass saw *The Graduate,* he was a junior in college, in 1967: "It was a time of great cultural change in the country. It was a very influential movie for me—the idea of what to do with my life, realizing there were choices out there. I didn't have strong career goals as a young person. I did not have a strong sense of direction. I really did feel the [Dustin Hoffman] character captured what I was going through."

On a broader cultural level, Glass responded to Paul Haggis's 2005 Academy Award winner: "*Crash* really captured a major issue in America . . . the multicultural collisions that we have in cities and even in small towns. Someone who was a hero one day was a villain the next day. The idea of good guys and bad guys . . . there are a lot of gray areas there."

Doris Kearns Goodwin *Biographer*

Two biopics have special resonance for Doris Kearns Goodwin, because they cover important eras in American history that she has written about. Having won her Pulitzer Prize for *No Ordinary Time: Franklin and Eleanor Roosevelt—The Home Front in World War II,* the writer picks Franklin J. Schaffner's *Patton* as Hollywood's best biopic.

"The film takes this character and shows his incredible pride and discipline, and how he brought the army up to an extraordinary level," says Goodwin. "And then it shows how he undoes himself because of those same qualities. He slaps soldiers and falls into disgrace and is made to apologize, but somehow is able to bring himself back to glory with the German siege at the end."

Released during the height of the Vietnam War, in 1970, *Patton* thrilled the hawks but also won fans among the doves, who thought George C. Scott captured the general's psychotic edge. Goodwin recalls how the film found devotees in both camps: "It was springtime, and Ted Williams was a batting coach for the Red Sox, and he was reading a book on [Gen. Douglas] MacArthur. He asked me, 'I suppose you hate MacArthur and Patton?' He jokingly called me a pinko. He assumed that liberals would hate both these men."

Whatever Goodwin thought of the man Patton, she definitely did like the movie: "That's because the film *Patton* made him into a human being with both sides. It was successful in creating a living human being with warts and strengths. And of course there was George C. Scott's performance!"

The author of *Team of Rivals: The Political Genius of Abraham Lincoln* also admires *Glory*.

"It's important in its depiction of Col. Robert Gould Shaw," she says, referring to the historic character played by Matthew Broderick. "Ed Zwick did an extraordinary job of showing the exploits of the black soldiers. People didn't know of their courage and what they had to go through to fight the battle at Fort Wagner. It's a story with an arc; from the beginning you see the unfairness against the black soldiers in terms of pay and equipment, and yet they melded together to perform spectacularly to help win the battles for the North."

The biographer calls the film "an important education for this country" and is often reminded of the movie's impact when she goes home to Boston. "Shaw's monument is on Beacon Street, right across from the State House. You can see the street where the parade took place, and I always think of that scene in the movie when I go there."

When writing her own Lincoln biography, Goodwin found herself influenced, for better or worse, by Hollywood's most popular movie.

"For a young girl, there was nothing like *Gone With the Wind*," says the writer:

> The summer I read it, I was thirteen and sat on blankets on
> the lawn with a friend, and we read that book all summer
> long. Then I saw the movie, which captured, if not surpassed,

the book. It is true when I wrote about Lincoln and the Civil War, the scenes from that movie were still in my head, even though I had learned how unbalanced it was to the [South's] side. The romance of the Civil War was set by *Gone With the Wind,* which makes slavery into something positive. People still romance that war. No other film had that effect on me.

And it wasn't just politics or history. Clark Gable's Rhett Butler, of course, "became the most desired man in life," Goodwin recalls. "And I used to worry if I was Melanie or Scarlett. I wanted to be like Scarlett but felt I was nicer than Scarlett and so I could, unfortunately, be Melanie."

Margaret Mitchell's heroine, at least in the person of Vivien Leigh, holds a special attraction for the young, in Goodwin's opinion: "The survival instinct is so strong in her, even if you don't like what she does to survive. When I look back on it now, Scarlett became the heroine rather than the ever-good Melanie, which suggests that there's something about desire and passion and ambition when you're young. You're drawn to it much more than to the person who gives everything and dies."

In the end, *Gone With the Wind* didn't turn Goodwin into an historian. "But it did figure into my ideals of romance and the grand, epic sweep of history," she believes.

Michael Govan *CEO and Director, Los Angeles County Museum of Art*

Michael Govan saw Stanley Kubrick's *2001: A Space Odyssey* at age five, and "Those images forever haunt me," Govan says. "My greatest interest in art is modern and abstract, light and space. *2001* had a big impact on my aesthetic."

He points to the final images of the 1968 sci-fi classic: "The monochromatic colors, the open space, the monolith, the abstract interiors, and even HAL, the circle that glows red. There is meaning and emotional content. These spaces which are devoid of decoration and yet have incredible meaning. This is what was going on in art at the time."

In high school, Govan toiled with becoming a computer programmer, and he later worked as an assistant editor on documentary films. "There was a point at which I asked myself, Did I want to go into museums or films? Both were creative endeavors. They are both a way to map out culture through images—film through narrative, museums through objects. Going to a museum can have a cinematic quality of light, space, objects, and walking through time.

"For me, it wasn't a particular movie about art that led me to [museums] but rather the incredible process of filmmaking that allows you to travel in time. It is not so different from hanging paintings so people can experience a landscape. It is cinematic."

Govan explains how curators in the nineteenth century often hung paintings in big frames with curtains on either side, lighting the art in darkened rooms to further reinforce the images. "The end of the nineteenth century was the great moment for grand landscape painting. What happened to landscape painting in the twentieth century?" he asks. "I make the case that landscape painting went into film. John Ford's *The Searchers,* for me, is one of the great landscape paintings. Ford owns Monument Valley in Utah. People could say that Jackson Pollock made the new landscape paintings."

Beyond the pure aesthetics, Govan also relates to Ford's message of history in the 1956 classic.

"The other aspect of *The Searchers* that makes it great is how it deals with the complexities of the West, especially racism and the genocide of the Native Americans," the LACMA director says. "Yet, it's also about the toughness of the American character and the heroic quality of these people."

Govan likes Westerns—"I'm from L.A.," he explains—and responds strongly to another oater from the mid-1950s, this one directed by Nicolas Ray in 1954 with two actresses, instead of guys,

The Searchers
John Wayne, 1956

duking it out with guns. "*Johnny Guitar* is very different from *The Searchers,*" he says. "It has a very modern feel to it, the gender-swapping. I love the roles of the two women [Joan Crawford, Mercedes McCambridge], who become so tough. It is a movie out of and for psychoanalysis. *Johnny Guitar* was assigned to me in an art class, because it plays on all this Freudian symbolism. Objects take on a psychological meaning, which had a huge impact on me."

Looking to how films have depicted the future, Govan applauds Ridley Scott's sci-fi movie from 1982. "The weirdly dystopian image of L.A. in *Blade Runner* seems weirdly plausible, if you think of Hong Kong and Tokyo and New York and world corporations," he says. "It is so contemporary regarding the issues of what is human. That is one of the most relevant issues in art right now: what defines 'human' in the age of manipulating DNA."

On the art front, Govan is not impressed with how Hollywood portrays artists.

"It's hard to profile an artist on film; the energy is in the work," he explains.

A notable exception for Govan is Robert Altman's *Vincent and Theo* from 1990, with Tim Roth and Paul Rhys standing in for Van Gogh and his put-upon brother. "It was an interesting way to explore those characters," says Govan, "to look at the personality of an artist through a double portrait, which kept the film away from being too heroic. It explored human character, but it was about art, too. I think Altman saw himself as an artist. There aren't many good art films. *The Agony and the Ecstasy* is fun. But it's hardly a deep psychological portrait of one of the most complex psychological artists."

Despite the film's camp status, Govan has occasionally found himself quoting from the 1965 biopic, directed by Carol Reed. It's the scene where Pope Julius II (Rex Harrison), frustrated over the long-delayed paint job in the Sistine Chapel, finally confronts Michelangelo (Charlton Heston).

"When will you make an end of it?" asks the pontiff.

"When I am finished!" says the painter.

"I like that exchange," says Govan.

Gore Vidal *Author*

Politics is in Gore Vidal's blood, both that which runs in his veins and that which runs through his work. As such, after watching Stephen Frears's film about Queen Elizabeth's contretemps with Prime Minister Tony Blair, he can't help but draw parallels to contemporary America.

"Does *The Queen* have any political message?" Vidal asks rhetorically. "Of course it does. It shows that there was once a generation that was brought up with the notion that we must serve.

A Midsummer Night's Dream
Jean Muir and Mickey Rooney, 1935

And Queen Elizabeth is quite lovely in that scene where she's explaining to Blair that she has her coronation oath, and her coronation oath is that she will serve until death. As for those who would like to see her abdicate so that poor Charles can have a chance, well, she swore an oath to remain on the job. She takes that seriously. And there's a great speech where Blair is saying, 'She's given her life to the country, and you want to trash her now?'

"Could you think of a similar situation in this country where anyone had ever done anything for anybody, or the country? Poor JFK started it with his inaugural address—he was trying to get everybody locked out of the 'me, me, me' mentality, which is all people ever think about. You ever talk to an American? Who do they talk about? Themselves."

But what most struck Vidal was the fact that *The Queen* saw Britain taking a hard look at its own history—an attempt he says most American filmmakers are loath to do.

"Anything grown-up like that we're never going to touch, and I believe it's starting to show up in our public life," he says. "I would think that things like *The Queen* would stimulate us. For God's sake, we've got figures, both female and male, who are far more interesting than Elizabeth II. No other country with a history as interesting as ours would have ignored Washington, Hamilton, Jefferson. If we hadn't, we would know more.

"It is to weep to watch *The Queen* and think of all the things of that nature we could be doing that we haven't done," he says of American movies.

Vidal has certainly never shied away from engaging American politics and history head-on. Growing up in Washington, D.C., with a senator for a grandfather, he went on to write political treatises too numerous to mention, as well as novels that retell American history (*Burr, Lincoln, Washington, D.C.*) and often take a revisionist view of doctrinal American figures (most notably Aaron Burr, whom Vidal attempted to rescue from the villains list of the Revolutionary period).

The Best Man, Vidal's 1960 stage play that he later adapted into a movie, was one of the first Hollywood films to cast a knowingly cynical eye on then-contemporary America's electoral machinations. It also bears an unfortunately serendipitous relation to history: a few years after *The Best Man* filmed a post-campaign-speech chase through the pantry of the Ambassador Hotel, Robert Kennedy was shot in the same room, under similar circumstances that Vidal finds "quite eerie."

Predictably, Vidal chose not to watch the re-creation of that event in Emilio Estevez's 2006 film, *Bobby*: "I saw the original in real life, and that was more than enough for me," he says.

Despite his track record with expostulatory novels and screenplays, Vidal professes no interest in tackling current U.S. dilemmas through fiction. Instead, he has opted for a series of firebrand polemics on the Bush administration, of which, to put it extremely mildly, he is no fan.

"Apparently everybody knows everything now; it's remarkable," he explains. "The more ignorant they are, the more positive they are. And these people you can't deal with, so I've stopped dealing with them entirely."

Never much of a twinkle-eyed optimist, Vidal sees little chance for film to cure the nation's ills: "No movie could ever counteract the actions of [the Bush] administration." Nor does he give a sunny prognosis for the industry itself: "Everyone on earth knows how much a certain picture costs and all the problems they had on location, but they have no interest in the movie. So we have a nation with brains like accountants; crooked ones, too."

The prolific writer gives two films credit for having changed his life. Max Reinhardt's and William Dieterle's 1935 classic, *A Midsummer Night's Dream,* which starred Mickey Rooney as Puck, turned Vidal on to the Bard: "I was ten, and I had never read Shakespeare much less seen one of his plays. I didn't just want to be Mickey Rooney; I wanted to be Mickey Rooney in *A Midsummer Night's Dream*. He could do anything as an actor, comedy or drama. By the age of fifteen, I had read all of Shakespeare's plays."

On the "less respectable" side of cinema, he mentions Karl Freund's 1932 horror film *The Mummy,* Boris Karloff's follow-up to *Frankenstein*. "I wanted to be an archeologist after that," Vidal recalls.

Surprisingly, he holds no apparent grudges regarding his own sometimes unpropitious encounters with Hollywood. "At least the disasters made from my work are far more famous than many people's successes," he reasons. "*Myra Breckinridge* being an example—it was about as bad as a movie could be. I thought my *Caligula* was quite a good script, but then it became a *Penthouse* picture and, well, we all know the rest."

ACKNOWLEDGMENTS

Variety executive editor/features Steven Gaydos conceived the "Gold Standard" feature (*Variety,* January 5, 2007) that led to this book, which he encouraged at all stages, and *Variety* editor in chief Peter Bart, publisher Neil Stiles, and Marci Sweren made it happen with their generous support.

On the book end, much thanks goes to Da Capo editors Jonathan Crowe, Adelaide Docx, and Collin Tracy; Eric Myers at the Joseph Spieler Agency; Photofest's Howard Mandelbaum; and *Variety*'s designers Danielle Grimes and Denise Smaldino.

—*Robert Hofler*

CONTRIBUTORS

To write this book, a number of *Variety* editors and contributors often split tasks. David Mermelstein and Holly Millea interviewed Christopher Hampton and Reese Witherspoon, respectively, and I wrote the profiles. Likewise, Stephen Schaefer interviewed Ben Affleck, Rosario Dawson, and Seth Rogen; Tobias Grey interviewed George Clooney and Tony Kushner. Stuart Levine wrote all profiles featured in Chapter 12 except for Gov. Bill Richardson's, which was written by Peter Debruge, and Ty Murray's, which was written by Andrew Barker. Debruge also wrote the profiles of Frank Cho, KAWS, and Jack Nicholson. Barker also contributed the profiles of James Cramer, Jamie Masada, Ellen Page, and Gore Vidal. Ryan Jimenez contributed the profiles of Eli Pariser and Dr. Drew Pinsky. Steven Gaydos wrote the Brad Bird profile. Anna Stewart contributed the profiles of Millie Martini Bratten, Raoul Felder, Dr. Brent D. Glass, Sen. John McCain, Isaac Mizrahi, Ralph Nader, Donald Trump, and Veronica Webb. Stewart and I collaborated on the profiles of Glenda Bailey, Candace Bushnell, Robert Downey Jr., Richard Gere, Anne Hathaway, Larry Madin, Sarah Jessica Parker, and Anne Rice. I wrote all other profiles. — *Robert Hofler*

INDEX